THE TRIADS OF BRITAIN

THE TRIADS OF BRITAIN

compiled by Iolo Morganwg

translated by W. Probert

with an Introduction and Glossary by Malcolm Smith

WILDWOOD HOUSE LONDON

First published 1977
Text Copyright © Bill Butler 1977
Illustrations Copyright © William MacLellan

Wildwood House Ltd,
29 King Street,
London WC2E 8JD

ISBN 0 7045 0290 9

IBM typeset by Supreme Litho Typesetting, Romford, Essex.
Printed and bound in Great Britain by Biddles Ltd, Guildford, Surrey.

CONTENTS

George Bain

INTRODUCTION

This collection of Triads was compiled by Iolo
Morganwg, or Edward Williams, the Georgian
antiquarian and poet. His original sources were not
disclosed by him; and, though the Triads themselves
seem to have been taken from a variety of sources,
the collection in its entirety plus many of the foot-
notes seem to have come from Morganwg's fertile
imagination.

Morganwg's inventions outdate by nearly a
century the better known Celtic studies of such
writers as W.B. Yeats, John Rhys, Lady Augusta
Gregory and A.E., and they are contemporary with
the compilations of Gaelic folktales made in the
Georgian period by T. Crofton Croker. The collec-
tion was first published as the 'Third Series of
Triads' in the *Myvyrian Archaiology of Wales*,
1801. It was translated circa 1823 by W. Probert.

Whether Morganwg adapted the Triads from oral
or unknown written tradition, or made them up
out of wholecloth, they parallel a number of other
writings. These include the early Welsh poems of
Taliesin, Aneurin and Llywarch Hen; The Mabino-
gion and Associated Stories; The Welsh Annals;
The Genealogies of the Welsh Princes and the
British Princes of North-West England and South

Scotland; the Histories of Nennius and Bede; materials contained in *The History of the Kings of Britain* by Geoffrey of Monmouth, and other twelfth century Arthurian literature, both British and Continental; the various lives of saints composed between the eighth and thirteenth centuries; Saxon chronicles and classical histories.

What is apparent from a reading of all of these is that they were inspired by common traditions which originate only partially in history and are otherwise mythological. Morganwg is, from a twentieth century viewpoint, no more 'spurious' than Geoffrey of Monmouth, Bede, Nennius or any of the other writers on this period, all of whom used embroidery when reality was deficient.

The Triads are called 'Welsh', although more properly they might be called 'British' because the peoples to which they refer are the Celtic races residing throughout the British Isles prior to the Saxon invasion of the fifth, sixth and seventh centuries. The literature of these peoples was less demotic than hieratic and may have been for the purpose of training a druidic priesthood during the period of the Roman occupation of Britain. However, with the Roman victory over the Druids on the island of Anglesey (Mona), the old religion was virtually exterminated; and with the Roman withdrawal from the British Isles in the early part of the fifth century came the simultaneous nascence of Christianity. Though Christianity is responsible in many cultures for the extermination of 'pagan' beliefs, in Britain as in Scandinavia it is Christian writers who preserved what little is known of the elder faiths. While in Iceland the Norse sagas survived Christianity largely by devices of plot, in Britain the Triads survived by means of their curious construction, which is implicit in the name 'Triads'; for each of these Triads is a triplet of related and parallel personages or subjects. This mnemonic trick, reinforced by the special sacredness among all Celtic peoples of the number three, facilitated memory and preserved a tradition long past the time it might otherwise have died.

The oldest surviving collections of this form date from the thirteenth century, although isolated instances may be found in early Welsh poems and prose literature. There is some evidence to show that the Triads are copies from manuscripts which may be dated to the eleventh century; but my guess is that the form evolved some time around the sixth and seventh centuries, perhaps earlier, and was then built on.

As exemplified here, each triad usually consists of an introductory line, stating the particular subject of the triad, i.e. 'There were three generous kings of the Isle of Britain', followed by examples: A, B and C. This brief formula was probably itself only an introduction to a more lengthy recital giving further details of lineage, location or instances of the subject matter; but with one or two exceptions the more elaborate details were not transcribed. (The commentaries in the present text are mostly those of Iolo Morganwg, and may have been intended by him to recreate a form which might have existed.) The Triads, then, as they have survived are only the tip of the iceberg, mnemonics or titles and paragraph-headings to refresh the memory of an 'extemporaneous' reciter; by general consent they appear to have originated in the bardic schools, and it may be fairly assumed that within these schools from a period *perhaps* as early as the Roman occupation and as late as the tenth century the Triads were intended to preserve an historical and exemplary tradition for use by the bards themselves and whoever may have been their successors, as well as to inspire some kind of national or cultural cohesion, patriotism if you will, among the Britons in the face of invasions by the Romans, the Saxons and the Christians.

The political geography of the period is more a matter for divination than for scholarship, as little written evidence has survived; for example, this collection of Triads is a late-eighteenth century agglomeration based upon writings of the thirteenth century and after, which are in turn founded on probable tenth or eleventh century written sources, which in their turn originate in traditions which appear to be at least half a millennium older, apparently almost entirely oral and apparently irrecoverable. The religion, Druidism, which was the genesis of the Triads, is written about by Caesar, Tacitus and other contemporary classical writers in such a way that people of the twentieth century end up knowing more of Caesar *et alia* than of the Druids.

It is certain that oak, mistletoe, the sickle and fire sacrifice played a part in druidic ritual, as verified by contemporary accounts. It is likely that the Druids made some religious use of such great monuments as Stonehenge; and it is even possible that the Druids, or their cultural forefathers, were responsible for the erection of these stone temples. Any other theory as to the religious belief of the Druids is strictly that, theory. The fragments of their culture are few and far between, tantalising glimpses of a culture which will probably remain to us virtually unknown. In *The Triads of Britain*, the settlement of the islands by the Celtic peoples, circa 600 B.C. and later, together with the stories of the early founders, culture heroes and law givers are set out in gnomic patterns. The Roman invasions of Julius Caesar (55 B.C. and 54 B.C.), the final years of Roman occupation, the histories of the 'British' Emperors, Magnus Maximus and Constantine, the loss of Britain to the Saxons and the histories of the Great Kings, Vortigern, Ambrosius and Arthur, are all part of the Triads. Though much of the material is legendary, it is the material of which history as well as dreams are made, and within this text one can see a rabble of warring Celtic tribes, conquered first by Rome, then by the Cross, and partially by the Saxons. Out of these invasions, and from the people who may first have sung these Triads, came the nation which is today Great Britain.

1977   MALCOLM SMITH

George Bain.

HERE WERE THREE NAMES GIVEN TO THE Isle of Britain from the first: before it was inhabited, it was called the Sea-girt Green Space; after it was inhabited, it was called the Honey Island; and after the people were formed into a common-wealth, by Prydain the son of Aedd the Great, it was denominated the Isle of Britain. And no one has any right to it but the tribe of the Cambrians, for they first took possession; and before that time were no persons living in it, but it was full of bears, wolves, crocodiles, and bisons.

2.   There were three primary divisions of the Isle of Britain: Cambria, Lloegria, and Alban, and the rank of sovereignty belongs to each of the three. And under a monarchy and voice of the country they are governed, according to the regulations of Prydain, the son of Aedd the Great; and to the nation of the Cambrians belongs the right of establishing the monarchy by the voice of the country and the people, according to rank and primeval right. And under the protection of such regulation, royalty ought to exist in every country in the Isle of Britain, and every royalty ought to

be under the protection of the voice of the country. Therefore it is said as a proverb:—

"A country is more powerful than a lord."

3. There are three pillars of the social state in the Isle of Britain: the voice of the country, royalty, and judicature, according to the regulation of Prydain the son of Aedd the Great.

4. There are three pillars of the nation of the Isle of Britain. The first was Hu the Mighty, who brought the nation of the Cambrians first to the Isle of Britain; and they came from the Summer Country, which is called Defrobani (that is, where Constantinople now stands); and they came over the Hazy Sea to the Isle of Britain, and to Armorica, where they settled. The second was Prydain the son of Aedd the Great, who first organised a social state and sovereignty in Britain; for before that time there was no justice but what was done by favour, nor any law, except that of superior force. The third was Dyvnwal Moelmud, for he first made arrangements respecting the laws, maxims, customs and privileges of the country and tribe. And on account of these reasons, they were called the three pillars of the nation of the Cambrians.

5. There were three social tribes of the Isle of Britain. The first was the tribe of the Cambrians, who came to the Isle of Britain with Hu the Mighty, because he would not possess a country and lands by fighting and pursuit, but by justice and tranquillity. The second was the tribe of the Lloegrians who came from Gascony; and they were descended from the primitive tribe of the

Cambrians. The third were the Brython, who came from Armorica, and who were descended from the primitive tribe of the Cambrians. These were called the three peaceful tribes, because they came by mutual consent and tranquility; and these tribes were descended from the primitive tribe of the Cambrians, and they had all three the same language and speech.

6.　There were three refuge-seeking tribes that came to the Isle of Britain; and they came under the peace and permission of the tribe of the Cambrians, without arms and without opposition. The first was the tribe of Caledonians in the north. The second was the Irish tribe, who dwell in the Highlands of Scotland. The third were the people of Galedin, who came in naked vessels to the Isle of Wight, when their country was drowned, and where they had land granted them by the tribe of the Cambrians. They had no privilege of claim in the Isle of Britain, but they had land and protection assigned to them under certain limitations; and it was stipulated that they should not possess the rank of native Cambrians until the ninth of their lineal descendants.

7.   There were three invading tribes that came to the Isle of Britain and who never departed from it. The first were the Coranians that came from the country of Pwyl. The second were Irish Picts who came to Alban by the North Sea. And the third were the Saxons. The Coranians are settled about the River Humber, and the shore of the German ocean; and the Irish Picts are in Alban about the shore of the sea of Denmark. The Coranians and Saxons united, and, by violence and conquest, brought the Lloegrians into confederacy with them; and subsequently took the crown of the monarchy from the tribe of the Cambrians. And there remained none of the Lloegrians that did not become Saxons, except those that are found in Cornwall, and in the commot of Carnoban in Deira and Bernicia. In this manner the primitive tribe of the Cambrians, who preserved both their country and their language, lost the sovereignty of the Isle of Britain on account of the treachery of the refuge-seeking tribes, and the pillage of the three invading tribes.

8.   There were three invading tribes that came to the Isle of Britain, and who subsequently left it. The first were the Scandinavians, who came here after Urb, with the Mighty Host, had taken away from the Island the flower of the tribe of the Cambrians. He took away with him 63,000 effective men, and steeds for war. And at the end of the third age, the Cambrians drove the Scandinavians over the sea into Germany. The second were the troops of Ganval the Irishman, that came into North Wales and settled there for twenty nine years, until they were driven into the sea by Caswallon the son of Beli and grandson of Mynogan. The third were the

Caesarians who continued by violence in this Island
more than four hundred years, when they returned
to Italy to oppose the fierce contention of the black
invasion; and they did not return again to the Isle
of Britain. And because the Cambrians marched
with them, none were left in the Island but women,
and little children under nine years of age.

9.   There were three treacherous invasions of the
Isle of Britain: the first were the red Irishmen from
Ireland, who came to Alban; the second were the
Scandinavians; and the third were the Saxons.
These last came to this Island in peace and by the
permission of the tribe of the Cambrians, and in
the protection of God and his truth, as well as in
the protection of the country and of the tribe; and
by treachery and mischief they opposed the tribe
of the Cambrians, and were able to wrest from
them the sovereign power of the Isle of Britain,
and they mutually confederated themselves in
Lloegria and Alban, where they still reside. This
happened in the age of Vortigern.

10.   There were three disappearances by loss in the
Isle of Britain. The first were Gavran and his men,
who went in search of the Green Islands of the
floods, and were never heard of after. The second
were Merddin the bard of Emrys, and his nine
attendant bards, who went to sea in a house of
glass, and the place where they went is unknown.
The third was Madog the son of Owain king of
North Wales, who went to sea with three hundred
persons in ten ships, but the place to which they
went is unknown.

11.   There were three oppressions that came upon
the Isle of Britain, but which were brought to a ter-
mination: first, the oppression of the horse of
Malaen, which is called the oppression of the first
of May; second, the oppression of the dragon of
Britain; and the oppression of the half-apparent
man. That is, the first was from beyond the sea; the
second was from the madness of the country and
nation under the pressure of the violence and
lawlessness of princes; but Dyvnwal Moelmud
destroyed it, by forming just regulations between
society and society, prince and neighbouring prince,
and country and neighbouring country; and the
third was in the time of Beli the son of Manogan,
which was a treacherous conspiracy, but he extin-
guished it.

12.   There were three frightful plagues in the Isle
of Britain. First, the plague that arose from the
corpses of the Irishmen who were slaughtered in
Manuba, after they had oppressed North Wales for
the space of twenty nine years. Second, the infec-
tion of the yellow plague of Rhoss, on account of
the corpses which were slain there, and if any one
went within reach of the effluvia he died immed-
iately. The third was the sickness of the Bloody
Sweat, on account of the corn having been
destroyed by wet weather in the time of the
Norman invasion by William the Bastard.

13.   There were three awful events in the Isle of
Britain. The first was the bursting of the Lake of
Floods, and the rushing of an inundation over all
the lands, until all persons were destroyed, except
Dwyvan and Dwyvach who escaped in an open
vessel; and from them the Isle of Britain was re-
peopled. The second was the trembling of the fiery
torrent, until the earth was rent to the abyss, and
the greatest part of all life was destroyed. The third
was the Hot Summer, when the trees and plants
took fire by the burning heat of the sun, and many
people and animals, various kinds of birds, vermin,
trees and plants, were entirely lost.

14.   There were three combined expeditions that
went from the Isle of Britain. The first was that
which went with Ur, the son of Erin, the
Bellipotent of Scandinavia; and he came to this
Island in the time of Gadial the son of Erin, to
solicit aid, under a condition that he should not
obtain from every principal fortress, a greater num-
ber than he should bring to it. To the first fortress
he only came himself with his servant Mathata
Vawr, and from there he obtained two, from the
second four, from the third eight, from the next
sixteen, and thus in like proportion from every
other fortress, until that in the last the number
could not be procured throughout the whole Island.
And he took with him 63,000, and he could not
obtain a greater number of effective men in all the
Island, and none but children and old men were
left behind. And Ur the son of Erin the Bellipotent
was the most complete levier that ever existed. It
was through inadvertency that the tribe of the
Cambrians gave him this permission under an irre-
vocable stipulation; and in consequence of this, the

Coranians found an opportunity to make an easy invasion of this island. Of the men who went, none ever returned, nor any of their progeny, nor descendants. They went on a warlike expedition as far as the sea of Greece, and remaining there in the land of Galas and Avena unto this day, they have become Greeks.

The second combined expedition was conducted by Caswallawn the son of Beli, and grandson of Manogan, and Gwenwynwyn and Gwanar the sons of Lliaws, the son of Nwyvre and Arianrod the daughter of Beli their mother. Their origin was from the border declivity of Galedin and Siluria, and from the combined tribes of the Boulognese; and their numbers were threescore and one thousand. They marched, with their uncle Caswallawn, after the Caesarians, unto the land of the Gauls of Armorica, who were descended from the primitive stock of the Cambrians. And none of them, nor of their progeny, returned to this island, for they settled in Gascony among the Caesarians, where they are at present; and it was in revenge of this expedition that the Caesarians came first into this Island.

The third combined expedition was marched out of this Island by Elen Bellipotent and Cynan her brother, lord of Meiriadog, to Armorica, where they obtained lands, power and sovereignty by the emperor Maximus for supporting him against the Romans. These men were from the land of Meiriadog, Siluria, and from the land of Gwyr and Gorwennydd; and none of them returned again, but settled there and in Ystre Gyvaelwg, where they formed a common-wealth. On account of this armed expedition, the tribe of the Cambrians became so deficient in armed men, that the Irish Picts invaded

them; and, therefore, Vortigern was forced to invite
the Saxons to expel the invasion. And the Saxons
observing the weakness of the Cambrians, treacher-
ously turned their arms against them, and by
combining with the Irish Picts and other traitors,
they took possession of the lands of the Cambrians,
and also their privileges and their crown. These
three combined expeditions are called the three
Mighty Presumptions of the tribe of the Cambrians,
and also the three Silver Armies, because they took
away from the Island all the gold and silver they
could obtain by deceit, artifice and injustice,
besides what they acquired by right and consent.
They are also called the three Unwise Armaments,
because they weakened the Island so much, that an
opportunity was given for the three Mighty
Invasions; namely, the Coranians, the Caesarians,
and the Saxons.

15.   There were three mighty invasions of the Isle
of Britain that united in one, and by this means the
invaders took from the Cambrians their rank, their
crown and their lands. The first was that of the
Coranians, who united with the Caesarians until
they became one. The second of the three were the
Caesarians. And the third were the Saxons, who
united with the two others against the Cambrians.
And God permitted this for the purpose of chastis-
ing the Cambrians for their three Mighty Presump-
tions, because they were carried into effect by
injustice.

16.　There were three primary tribes of the
Cambrians: the Gwentians, or the Silurians; the
Ordovices, including both the North Walians and
Powysians; and the tribe of Pendaran of Dyved,
including the people of Pembrokeshire, Gower and
Cardiganshire. To each of these belongs a classical
dialect of the Welsh language.

17.　There were three monarchs by the verdict of
the Isle of Britain: the first was Caswallawn the son
of Lludd, son of Beli, son of Mynogan; the second
was Caradog, son of Bran, son of Llyr Llediaith;
and the third was Owain the son of Maximus. That
is, sovereignty was conferred upon them by the
verdict of the country and the nation, when they
were not elders.

18.　There were three holy families in the Isle of
Britain. First, the family of Bran the blessed, the
son of Llyr Llediaith; for Bran was the first who
brought the faith of Christ to this Island from
Rome, where he was in prison through the treach-
ery of Boadicea, the daughter of Mandubratius the
son of Lludd. The second was the family of
Cynedda Wledig, who first gave land and privilege
to God and the saints in the Isle of Britain. The
third was Brychan of Brecknockshire, who educat-
ed his children and grandchildren in learning and
generosity, that they might be able to show the
faith in Christ to the Cambrians, where they were
without faith.

19.　There were three benignant guests of the Isle
of Britain: St. David, Padarn, and Teilaw. They
were so called because they went as guests into the
houses of the nobles, the yeomen, the native and

the bondman, without accepting either gift or
reward, food or drink; but they taught the faith in
Christ to every one without pay, or thanks, and to
the poor and the destitute they gave of their gold
and their silver, their clothes and their provisions.

20.   There were three treacherous meetings in the
Isle of Britain. First the meeting of Mandubratius
the son of Lludd, and the traitors with him, who
gave a place for the landing of the Romans on the
narrow Green Point, and not more; and the con-
sequence of which was, the gaining of the Island
by the Romans. The second was the meeting of
the Cambrian nobles and the Saxon Claimants upon
Salisbury Plain, where the plot of the Long Knives
took place through the treachery of Vortigern; for
by his counsel, in league with the Saxons, nearly
all the Cambrian nobility were slain. Third, the
meeting of Medrawd and Iddawg Corn Prydain with
their men in Nanhwynain, where they entered into
conspiracy against Arthur, and by this means
strengthened the Saxon cause in the Isle of Britain.

26

21.   The three arrant traitors of the Isle of Britain.
First Mandubratius, son of Llud, son of Beli the
Great, who invited Julius Caesar and the Romans
into this Island, and caused the invasion of the
Romans. That is, he and his men gave themselves
as guides to the Romans, and received a treasure of
gold and silver from them every year. In conse-
quence of this, the men of this Island were com-
pelled to pay three thousand pieces of silver every
year as a tribute to the Romans until the time of
Owain the son of Maximus, who refused to pay the
tribute. And under pretence of being content, the
Romans drew from the Isle of Britain the most
effective men who were capable of becoming soldiers,
and marched them to Aravia and other far countries,
from whence they never returned. And the Romans
who were in Britain went into Italy, and left only
women and little children behind them; and, there-
fore, the Britons were so weakened, that they were
not able to oppose invasion and conquest for want
of men and strength. The second was Vortigern,
who murdered Constantine the Blessed, seized the
crown of the Island by violence and lawlessness,
first invited the Saxons to the Island as his defend-
ers, married Alis Ronwen the daughter of Hengist,
and gave the crown of Britain to the son he had by
her, whose name was Gotta; and on this account,
the kings of London are called children of Alis.
Thus, on account of Vortigern, the Cambrians lost
their lands, their rank and their crown in Lloegria.
The third was Medrawd the son of Llew, the son of
Cynvarch: for when Arthur left the government of
the Isle of Britain in his custody, whilst he marched
against the Roman emperor, Medrawd took the
crown from Arthur by usurpation and seduction;
and in order to keep it, he confederated with the

Saxons; and, on this account, the Cambrians lost the crown of Lloegria and the sovereignty of the Isle of Britain.

22. The three secret treasons of the Isle of
Britain. First, the betraying of Caradog son of Bran
by Boadicea, daughter of Mandubratius, the son of
Lludd, and delivering him up a captive to the
Romans. Second, the betraying of Arthur by
Iddawg Corn Prydain, who divulged his designs.
And third, the betraying of Prince Llywelyn, son
of Grufudd, by Madog Min. By these three treach-
eries the Cambrians were completely subdued; and
nothing but treachery could have overcome them.

23. The three heroic sovereigns of the Isle of
Britain: Cunobelinus, Caradog the son of Bran, and
Arthur; because they conquered their enemies, and
could not be overcome but by treachery and
plotting.

24. The three primary battle princes of the Isle
of Britain: Caswallawn the son of Beli, Gweirydd
the son of Cunobelinus, and Caradog, the son of
Bran, son of Llyr Llediaith.

25. The three accomplished princes of the Isle of
Britain: Rhun the son of Maelgwn; Owain, the son
of Urien; and Rhuvon the Fair, son of Dewrath
Wledig.

26. There were three plebeian princes in the Isle
of Britain: Gwrgai, son of Gwrien in the North;
Cadavael son of Cynvedw in North Wales; and
Hyvaidd the Tall son of St. Bleiddan, in Glamorgan.
That is to say, sovereignty was granted them on
account of their heroic actions, and virtuous
qualities.

27.   The three banded families of the Isle of
Britain: the family of Caswallawn with the Long
Hand; the family of Rhiwallon, son of Urien; and
the family of Belyn of Lleyn. They were so called,
because they were not subject to either head, or
sovereign, as it respected the rank of their families
and power, but owed submission only to the voice
of the country and the nation.

28.   The three golden-banded-ones of the Isle of
Britain: Rhiwallon with the Broom Hair; Rhun, the
son of Maelgwn; and Cadwaladyr the Blessed. That
is, they were permitted to wear golden bands about
their arms, their necks and their knees; and with
these was granted the privilege of royalty in every
country and dominion in the Isle of Britain.

29.   The three battle-knights of the sovereign of
the Isle of Britain: Caradog with the brawny arm;
Llyr the Bellipotent; and Mael, the son of
Menwaed, of Arllechwedd. And with reference to
these, Arthur composed the following lines:—
      These are my three battle-knights,
      Mael the Tall, and Llyr the Bellipotent,
      And Caradog the pillar of the Cambrians.
That is to say, they were the bravest heroes of all
battle-knights, and therefore royalty was granted
them, and what they wished of power; and their
courtesy was such, that they would do nothing but
what was judicious and right, in whatever country
they came.

30.   The three generous princes of the Isle of
Britain: Rhydderch the Generous, son of Tudwal
Tudclud; Mordav the Generous, son of Servan; and
Nudd the Generous, son of Senyllt. Their courteous
dispositions were such, that they did not fail to
grant any thing whatever to any person who solicited
it of them, if they had it in possession, or could
obtain it by gift, loan, or present, whether the
applicants were friends or foes, relatives or
strangers.

31.   The three blood-stained ones of the Isle of
Britain: Arthur, Morgan the Greatly Courteous, and
Rhun, the son of Beli. When they marched to war,
no one could stay at home, so greatly were they
beloved; and in every war and battle, they were
victorious, where there was neither treachery, nor
ambush. Hence arose the proverb:— "There were
three heroes who obtained men wherever they
marched: Arthur, Morgan the Greatly Courteous,
and Rhun the son of Beli; and there were three
armies who obtained soldiers wherever they
marched: the soldiers of Arthur, the soldiers of
Morgan the Greatly Courteous, and the troops of
Rhun, the son of Beli."

32.   The three resolute minded ovates of the Isle
of Britain: Greidiawl the resolute minded ovate,
Envael the son of Adran, and Trystan, the son of
Tallwch; for they had the privilege of going
wherever they wished in the Isle of Britain without
opposition, unless they went unlawfully.

33.   The three obstructors of slaughter of the Isle
of Britain: Grudnew, Henben, and Eidnew. Their
principle was, not to retreat from battle and con-
flict but upon their biers, after they were unable to
move either hand or foot.

34.   The three conventional monarchs of the Isle
of Britain: first, Prydain, son of Aedd the Great,
when there was established a discriminating sove-
reignty over the Isle of Britain, and its adjacent
islands; second, Caradog, the son of Bran, when he
was elected Generalissimo of all the Island of
Britain to oppose the incursions of the Romans;
and Owain, the son of Ambrosius, when the
Cambrians resumed the sovereignty from the
Roman emperor, according to the rights of the
nation. These were called the three conventional
sovereigns, because they were raised to this dignity
by the convention of the country and the bordering
country, within all the limits of the nation of the
Cambrians, by holding a convention in every
district, commot, and hundred in the Isle of Britain
and its adjacent islands.

35. The three blessed princes of the Isle of
Britain. First, Bran the Blessed, the son of Llyr
Llediaith, who first brought the faith of Christ to
the Cambrians from Rome, where he had been
seven years as a hostage for his son Caradog, whom
the Romans put in prison, after being betrayed
through the enticement, deceit and plotting of
Boadicea. Second, Lleirwg, son of Coel, son of St.
Cyllin, and called Lleuver the Great, who built the
first church in Llandav, which was the first in the
Isle of Britain, and who gave the privilege of the
country and tribe, with civil and ecclesiastical
rights, to those who professed faith in Christ. The
third was Cadwaladyr the Blessed, who gave protec-
tion, within his lands and within all his possessions,
to the Christians who fled from the infidel and law-
less Saxons who wished to murder them.

36. The three system formers of royalty of the
Isle of Britain: Prydain the son of Aedd the Great,
Dyvnwal Moelmud, and Bran the son of Llyr
Llediaith. That is, their systems were the best
systems of royalty of the Isle of Britain, and they
were judged superior to all other systems which
were formed in the Isle of Britain.

37. The three disgraceful drunkards of the Isle of
Britain. First, Ceraint, the drunken king of Siluria,
who in drunkenness burnt all the corn far and near
over all the country, so that a famine for bread
arose. Second, Vortigern, who in his drink gave the
Isle of Thanet to Horsa that he might commit
adultery with Rowena his daughter, and who also
gave a claim to the son that he had by her to the
crown of Lloegria; and added to these, treachery
and plotting against the Cambrians. Third, the

drunken Seithynin, son of Seithyn Saida king of
Dimetia, who in his drunkenness let the sea over
the hundred of Gwaelod so that all the houses and
land which were there, were lost; where before that
event sixteen fortified towns were reckoned there,
superior to all the towns and fortified stations in
Cambria, with the exception of Caerllion upon Usk.
The hundred of Gwaelod was the dominion of
Gwydnaw Garanhir, king of Cardigan. This event
happened in the time of Ambrosius. The people
who escaped from that inundation landed in
Ardudwy, and the country of Arvon, and the
mountains of Snowdon, and other places, which
had not been inhabited before that period.

38.   The three humble princes of the Isle of
Britain: Manawyda son of Llyr Llediaith, after
Bran the son of Llyr, his brother, was carried into
captivity; Llywarch the Aged, son of Elidir
Llydanwyn; and Gwgon the Hero, the son of
Eleuver with the Mighty Retinue. These three were
bards; and after they had attached themselves to
song, they sought not for dominion and royalty,
though no one could debar them from it. On this
account, they were called the three humble princes
of the Isle of Britain.

39.   The three chiefs of Deira and Bernicia: Gall
the son of Dysgyvedog; Difedel the son of
Dysgyvedog; and Ysgavnell the son of Dysgyvedog.
These three were the sons of bards, and after they
had attached themselves to song, the sovereignty
of Deira and Bernicia was bestowed upon them.

40.   The three bards of the Isle of Britain who tinged spears with blood: Tristvardd, son of Urien Rheged; Dygynnelw the bard of Owain son of Urien; and Avan Verddig, bard of Cadwallon son of Cadvan. These three were sons of bards, and they could not be separated.

41.   The three supreme servants of the Isle of Britain: Caradog, the son of Bran, the son of Llyr Llediaith; Cawrdav, the son of Caradog with the Brawny Arm; and Owain, the son of Ambrosius. They were so called because all the men of the Island of Britain, from the prince to the peasant, became their followers at the need of the country, on account of the invasion and tyranny of the foe. And wherever these three marched to war, there was not a man in the Isle of Britain but who would join their armies, and would not stay at home. And these three were the sons of bards.

42.   The three fetter-wearing kings of the Isle of Britain: Morgan the Greatly Courteous, of Glamorgan; Elystan Glodrydd, between the Wye and the Severn; and Gwaithvoed, king of Cardigan. They were so called because they wore fetters in all their primary functions of royalty in the Isle of Britain instead of frontlets or crowns.

43.   The three frontlet-wearing kings of the Isle of Britain: Cadell, king of Dinevor; Anarawd, king of Aberfraw; and Mervin, king of Mathravael. They were also called the three frontlet-wearing princes.

44.   The three foreign kings of the Isle of Britain: Gwrddyled of the Conflict; Morien with the Beard; and Constantine the Blessed.

45.   The three disgraceful traitors who enabled
the Saxons to take the crown of the Isle of Britain
from the Cambrians. The first was Gwrgi Garwlwyd,
who, after tasting human flesh in the court of
Edelfled the Saxon king, became so fond of it that
he would eat no other but human flesh ever after.
In consequence of this, he and his men united with
Edelfled king of the Saxons; and he made secret
incursions upon the Cambrians, and brought a
young male and female whom he daily ate. And all
the lawless men of the Cambrians flocked to him
and the Saxons, where they obtained their full of
prey and spoil taken from the natives of this Isle.
The second was Medrod, who with his men united
with the Saxons, that he might secure the kingdom
to himself, against Arthur; and in consequence of
that treachery many of the Lloegrians became as
Saxons. The third was Aeddan, the traitor of the
North, who with his men made submission to the
power of the Saxons, so that they might be able to
support themselves by confusion and pillage under
the protection of the Saxons. On account of these
three traitors the Cambrians lost their land and their
crown in Lloegria; and if it had not been for such
treasons, the Saxons could not have gained the
Island from the Cambrians.

46.   The three bards who committed the three
beneficial assassinations of the Isle of Britain. The
first was Gall, the son of Dysgyvedawg, who killed
the two brown birds of Gwendolleu, the son of
Ceidiaw, that had a yoke of gold about them, and
that daily devoured two bodies of the Cambrians
for their dinner and two for their supper. The
second was Ysgavnell, the son of Dysgyvedawg,
who killed Edelfled king of Lloegria, who required

every night two noble maids of the Cambrian
nation, and violated them, and every morning he
killed and devoured them. The third was Difidel,
the son of Dysgyvedawg, who killed Gwrgi
Garwlwyd, that had married Edelfled's sister, and
committed treachery and murder in conjunction
with Edelfled upon the Cambrians. And this Gwrgi
killed a Cambrian male and female every day and
devoured them, and on the Saturday he killed two
males and two females, that he might not kill on
the Sunday. And these three persons, who per-
formed these beneficial assassinations, were bards.

47.   The three infamous assassinations of the Isle
of Britain: the assassination of Aneurin of flowing
muse and monarch of the bards, by Eiddin the son
of Einygan; the assassination of Avaon, the son of
Taliesin, by Llawgad Trwm Bargawd; and the
assassination of Urien, the son of Cynvarch, by
Llovan Llaw Dino. They were three bards who were
assassinated by these three men.

48.   The three infamous blows with the axe of the
Isle of Britain: the axe-blow of Eiddin, the son of
Einygan, on the head of Aneurin of flowing muse;
the axe-blow of Cadavael the Wild, on the head of
Jago, the son of Beli; and the axe-blow upon the
head of Golyddan the bard, because of the stroke
which he gave Cadwaladyr the Blessed with the
palm of his hand.

49.   The three fatal slaps of the Isle of Britain:
the slap of Matholwch the Irishman, on Bronwen
the daughter of Llyr; the slap which Gwenhwyvach
gave Gwenhwyvar, and which caused the battle of
Camlan; and the slap which Golyddan the bard
gave Cadwaladyr the Blessed.

50.   The three frivolous causes of battle in the
Isle of Britain. The first was the battle of Goddeu,
which was caused about a bitch, a roe-buck and a
lapwing; and in that battle 71,000 men were slain.
The second was the action of Arderydd, caused by
a bird's nest, in which 80,000 Cambrians were
slain. The third was the battle of Camlan, between
Arthur and Medrod, where Arthur was slain with
100,000 of the choice men of the Cambrians. On
account of these three foolish battles, the Saxons
took the country of Lloegria from the Cambrians,
because there was not a sufficient number of
warriors left to oppose the Saxons, the treachery
of Gwrgi Garwlwyd, and the deception of
Eiddilic the dwarf.

51.   The three fatal counsels of the Isle of Britain.
First, to give permission to Julius Caesar and the
Romans with him, to have a place for the fore-
hoofs of their horses in the cave of the verdant
edge in the Isle of Thanet, because by this the
Caesarians obtained a landing place to take posses-
sion of the Isle of Britain, and to form a junction
with the traitor Mandubratius the son of Lludd.
Such permission was granted to the Caesarians
because the Cambrians thought it contemptible to
defend their country otherwise than through
strength of arms, heroism, and the bravery of the

arthur
Bran

people, where they had no suspicion of the treachery of Mandubratius, the son of Lludd, with the Romans. The second fatal counsel was that of permitting Horsa, Hengist and Rowena to return to the Isle of Britain, after they were driven over the sea to the country from whence they originated. And the third was to suffer Arthur to divide his men with Medrawd three times in the battle of Camlan, and through which Arthur lost the victory and his life, where Medrawd was united with the Saxons.

52.   The three tremendous slaughters of the Isle of Britain. The first, when Medrawd went to Galliwig, he did not leave in the court meat and drink to support a fly, but consumed and wasted it all; and he pulled Gwenhwyvar from her throne, and committed adultery with her. The second was, when Arthur went to the court of Medrawd, he left neither meat nor drink that he did not destroy; and killed every living thing in the hundred, both man and beast. The third was, when the traitorous Aeddan went to the court of Rhydderch the Generous, he destroyed all the meat and drink in the court, without leaving as much as would feed a fly; and he did not leave either a man or beast alive, but destroyed the whole. These were called the three dreadful slaughters because the Cambrians were compelled, according to law and custom, to answer and grant redress for what was done in that irregular, unusual, and lawless manner.

53.   The three concealments and disclosures of the Isle of Britain. The first was the head of Bran the Blessed, the son of Llyr, that Owain the son of Ambrosius had concealed in the white hill in

London; and whilst it remained in that state, no
injury could happen to this Island. The second were
the bones of Gwrthevyr the Blessed, which were
buried in the principal ports of the Island, and while
they remained there no molestation could happen to
to this Island. The third were the dragons which
were concealed by Lludd the son of Beli in the for-
tress of Pharaon among the rocks of Snowdon. And
these three concealments were placed under the
protection of God and his attributes, so that misery
should fall upon the hour and the person who
should disclose them. Vortigern revealed the
dragons out of revenge for the opposition of the
Cambrians towards him, and he invited the Saxons
under the semblance of auxiliaries to fight with the
Irish Picts; and after that, he revealed the bones of
Gwrthevyr the Blessed out of love to Rowena the
daughter of Hengist the Saxon. And Arthur revealed
the head of Bran the Blessed, the son of Llyr,
because he scorned to keep the Island but by his
own might; and after these three disclosures, the
invaders obtained the superiority over the Cambrian
nation.

54.   The three over-ruling counter energies of the Isle of Britain: Hu the Mighty, who brought the Cambrian nation from the Summer Country, called Defrobani, unto the Isle of Britain; Prydain, the son of Aedd the Great, who organised the nation and established a jury over the Isle of Britain; and Rhitta Gawr, who made a robe for himself of the beards of those kings whom he made captives, on account of their oppression and lawlessness.

55.   The three beneficial harassers of the Isle of Britain: Prydain, the son of Aedd the Great, harassing the dragon of oppression, which was the oppression of pillage and lawlessness, engendered in the Isle of Britain; Caradog, the son of Bran, the son of Llyr, harassing the Roman invaders; and Rhitta Gawr, harassing the oppression and pillaging of dissolute kings.

56.   The three benefactors of the Cambrian nation. First, Hu the Mighty, who first taught the Cambrians the way to plough, when they were in the Summer Country, before they came to the Isle of Britain. Second, Coll, the son of Collvrewi, who first brought wheat and barley to the Isle of Britain, for before that time there was nothing but oats and rye. Third, Elldud, the holy knight of Theodosius, who improved the mode of ploughing land and taught the Cambrians better than was known before, and he gave them the system and art of cultivating lands as is used at present; for before that time land was cultivated only with the mattock and over-tread plough, after the manner of the Irish.

57.   The three primary inventors of the Cambrians. Hu the Mighty, who formed the first mote and

retinue over the nation of Cambria; Dyvnwal Moelmud, who made the first regulations of the laws, privileges and customs of the country and tribe; and Tydain, the father of poetic genius who made the first order and regulation for the record and memorial of vocal song, and that which appertains to it. From this system, the privileges and organised customs, respecting the bards and bardism in the Isle of Britain, were first formed.

58.   The three primary bards of the Isle of Britain: Plennydd, Alawn, and Gwron. That is, these formed the privileges and customs that appertain to bards and bardism, and therefore they are called the three primary bards. Nevertheless, there were bards and bardism prior to them, but they had not a licensed system, and they had neither privileges nor customs otherwise than what they obtained through kindness and civility, under the protection of the nation and the people, before the time of these three. (Some say that these lived in the time of Prydain, the son of Aedd the Great, but others affirm that they flourished in the time of Dyvnwal Moelmud's son; and this information they derive from ancient manuscripts which are entitled 'Dyvnwarth the son of Prydain'.)

59. The three beneficial sovereigns of the Isle of Britain. First, Prydain, the son of Aedd the Great, who first formed a system of citizenship of the country and tribe, and the organisation of the country and the bordering country in the Isle of Britain. Second, Dyvnwal Moelmud, who improved and extended the institutes, laws, privileges and customs of the Cambrian nation, so that equity and justice might be obtained by all in the Isle of Britain, under the protection of God and his tranquillity, and under the protection of the country and the tribe. Third, Howel the Good, son of Cadell, and grandson of Rhodri the Great, king of all Cambria, who improved the laws of the Isle of Britain, as the changes and circumstances which occurred among the Cambrians demanded, lest what was good might be effaced, and lest what was excellent might not succeed it, according to the conditions and effect of the organisation of the Cambrians. And these three men were the best of legislators.

60. The three vigorous ones of the Isle of Britain: Gwrnerth the sharp shot, who killed the greatest bear that was ever seen with a straw arrow; Gwgawn with the mighty hand, who rolled the stone of Maenarch from the valley to the summit of the mountain, and which required sixty oxen to draw it there; and Eidiol the Mighty, who, in the plot of Stonehenge, killed six hundred and sixty Saxons with a billet of the service tree, between sun-set and dark.

61. The three royal families that were conducted to prison from the great great grandfather to the great grandchildren, without permitting one of

them to escape. First, the family of Llyr Llediaith, who were put in prison in Rome, by the Caesarians. Second, the family of Madawg son of Medron, who were imprisoned in Alban, by the Irish Picts. Third, the family of Gair son of Geirion, who were imprisoned in Oeth and Anoeth, by the verdict of the country and tribe. Not one, nor another of these escaped; and it was the most complete incarceration that was ever known, with respect to these families.

62. The three archbishopricks of the Isle of Britain. First, Llandav, through the favour of Lleirwg son of Coel and grandson of Cyllin, who first gave lands and the privilege of the country to those who first dedicated themselves to the faith in Christ. Second, York, through the favour of the emperor Constantine; for he was the first of the Roman emperors who embraced the Christian religion. The third was London, through the favour of the emperor Maximus. Afterwards there were Caerllion upon Usk, Celliwig in Cornwall, and Edinburgh in the North; and now there are St. David's, York, and Canterbury.

63. The three supreme thrones of the Isle of Britain: first, London; second, Caerllion upon Usk; and third, York.

48

64. The three tribes of the throne of the Isle of Britain. The first is Caerllion upon Usk; and there Arthur has supreme authority, St. David son of Cunedda Wledig being chief bishop, and Maelgwyn of North Wales being chief elder. Second, Celliwig in Cornwall, and there Arthur has supreme authority, Bedwini being chief bishop, and Caradawg with the Brawny Arm chief elder. Third, Edinburgh in the North; and there Arthur has supreme authority, Cyndeyrn Garthwys being chief bishop, and Gwrthmwl Wledig chief elder.

65. The three privileged ports of the Isle of Britain: Newport in Monmouthshire, Beaumaris in Anglesea, and Gwyddnaw in Cardiganshire.

66. The three most noted rivers of the Isle of Britain: the Severn in Cambria, the Thames in Lloegria, and the Humber in Deira and Bernicia.

67. The three primary Islands attached to the Isle of Britain: Orkney, Man, and Wight. At a subsequent period the sea broke through the land, and Anglesea became an Island; and in a similar manner the Orkney Isle was broken, and many Islands were formed in consequence, and other parts of Scotland and Cambria became Islands.

68. The three fleet-owners of the Isle of Britain: Geraint the son of Erbin; Gwenwynwyn the son of Nav; and March the son of Meirchion. Each of these admirals had one hundred and twenty ships, and one hundred and twenty sailors in each ship.

69.   The three frontlet ones of battle of the Isle
of Britain: Trystan, son of Tallwch; Huail, son of
Caw of Prydyn, lord of the vale of Cawlwyd; and
Cai, son of Cynyr with the Shining Beard. And
there was one frontlet wearer above the other
three, who was Bedwyr, the son of Pedrawg.

70.   The three naturalists of the Isle of Britain:
Gwalchmai the son of Gwyar; Llecheu son of
Arthur; and Rhiwallon of the Broom-brush-hair;
and there was nothing of which they did not know
its material essence, and its property, whether of
kind, part, quality, compound, coincidence,
tendency, nature, or of essence, whatever it
might be.

71.   The three pillars of battle of the Isle of
Britain: Dunawd Fur son of Pabo the Pillar of
Britain; Gwallawg son of Lleenawg; and Cynvelyn
the Stumbler. That is, they understood the order
and necessary arrangements for battle better than
any others that ever existed.

72.   The three bulls of battle of the Isle of Britain:
Cynvar Cadgadawg son of Cynwyd Cynwydion;
Gwendolleu son of Ceidiaw; and Urien son of
Cynvarch; because they rushed upon their foes like
bulls, and it was not possible to avoid them.

73.   The three bull princes of the Isle of Britain:
Elmur the adopted son of Cibddar; Cynhaval son of
Argad; and Avaon son of Taliesin, chief of the
bards. These three were bards; and they dreaded
nothing in battle and conflict, but rushed forward,
regardless of death.

74.   The three arrogant ones of the Isle of Britain:
Sawyl the lofty headed; Pasgen the son of Urien;
and Rhun the son of Einiawn. Their arrogance was
most arrogant above every other arrogant thing, by
means of which they brought anarchy in the Isle
of Britain; and those who were influenced by this
anarchy, united with the Saxons, and finally
became Saxons.

75.   The three strong crutched ones of the Isle of
Britain: Rhineri son of Tangwn; Tinwaed the
crutched; and Pryderi son of Doler of Deira and
Bernicia.

76.   The three grave slaughterers of the Isle of
Britain: Selyv son of Cynan Garwyn; Avaon son of
Taliesin; and Gwallawg son of Lleenawg. They were
called grave slaughterers because they were able to
avenge their wrongs from their graves.

77.   The three golden-corpses of the Isle of
Britain: Madawg the son of Brwyn; Ceugant
Beilliawg: and Rhuvon the Fair, son of Gwyddnaw
Garanhir. They are so called because their weight
in gold was given to deliver them from those who
slew them.

78.   The three forward ones of the Isle of Britain:
Eiddilic the dwarf; Trystan the son of Tallwch; and
Gweirwerydd the Great; because there was nothing
could divert them from their designs.

51

79.   The three generous hosts of the Isle of
Britain: the host of Belyn son of Cynvelyn, in the
warfare of Caradawg son of Bran; the host of
Mynyddawg Eiddin in the battle of Cattraeth; and
the host of Drywon son of Nudd the Generous, in
the defile of Arderydd in the North. That is, every
one marched at his own expense, without waiting
for being summoned, and without demanding
either pay or reward of the country, or the prince;
and because of this they are called the three
generous hosts.

80.   The three loyal tribes of the Isle of Britain.
The tribe of Cadwallawn the adopted son of Cadvan,
who were with him seven years in Ireland, and dur-
ing that time they demanded neither pay, nor
reward, lest they should be obliged to leave him,
and he should not be able to make the compensa-
tion to which they were entitled. Second, the tribe
of Gavran son of Aeddan, when the loss by
disappearance took place, who went to sea in
search of their lord. Third, the family of
Gwendolleu son of Ceidiaw, who maintained the
battle forty six days after their lord was slain. The
number of each of these tribes was twenty one
hundred heroic men, and so great was their courage
that they could not be vanquished.

81.　The three disloyal tribes of the Isle of Britain.
The tribe of Goronwy the Fair from Penllyn, who
refused to stand instead of their lord to receive the
poisoned javelin from Llew Llaw Gyfes by the
Stone of Goronwy before Cynvel, in Ardudwy. The
tribe of Gwrgi and Peredur who deserted their lords
in the fortress of Crau, where there was an appoint-
ment for battle the next morning with Ida the Great
Knee, and they were both slain. The third were the
tribe of Alan Morgan, who returned back from their
lord by stealth, leaving him and his servants to
march to Camlan, where he was slain.

82.　Three things that caused the reduction of
Lloegria and wrested it from the Cambrians: the
harbouring of strangers, the liberating of prisoners,
and the present of the Bald Man.

83.　The three men who escaped from the battle
of Camlan: Morvran son of Tegid who, being so
ugly, every one thought he was the devil from hell
and fled before him; Sandde Angel-aspect, who
having so fine a shape, so beautiful, and so lovely,
that no one raised an arm against him, thinking that
he was an angel from heaven; and Glewlwyd with
the Mighty Grasp, for so large was his size and
mighty his strength, that no one could stand before
him, and every one fled at his approach. These are
the three men who escaped from the battle of
Camlan.

54

84.   The three chief perpetual choirs of the Isle of Britain: the choir of Llan Illtyd Vawr, Glamorganshire; the choir of Ambrosius in Ambresbury; and the choir of Glastonbury. In each of these three choirs there were 2,400 saints; that is, there were a hundred for every hour of the day and the night in rotation, perpetuating the praise and service of God without rest or intermission.

85.   The three shepherd retinues of the Isle of Britain: Benren the herdsman in Gorwennydd, who kept the herd of Caradawg son of Bran and his retinue, and in which herd there were 21,000 milch cows. Second, Gwydion son of Dôn, who kept the cattle of the tribe of North Wales above the Conway, and in that herd were 21,000. Third, Llawvrodedd the knight, who tended the cattle of Nudd the Generous, son of Senyllt, and in that herd were 21,000 milch cows.

86.   The three roving fleets of the Isle of Britain: the fleet of Llawr son of Eidriv; the fleet of Divwg son of Alban; and the fleet of Dolor son of Mwrchath, king of Manaw.

87.   The three chief cities of the Isle of Britain: Caerllion upon Usk in Cambria; London in Lloegria; and York in Deira and Bernicia.

George Bain

88.   The three mighty achievements of the Isle of Britain: raising the stone of Ceti; erecting Stonehenge; and heaping the pile of Cyvrangon.

89.   The three renowned astronomers of the Isle of Britain: Idris the giant; Gwydion son of Dôn; and Gwyn son of Nudd. Such was their knowledge of the stars, their natures and qualities, that they could prognosticate whatever was wished to be known unto the day of doom.

90.   The three illusive and half-apparent men of the Isle of Britain: Math son of Mathonwy, who showed his illusion to Gwydion son of Dôn; Menw the son of Teirgwaedd, who revealed his secret to Uthyr Pendragon; and Rhuddlwm the giant, who revealed his secret to Eiddilic the dwarf, and Coll son of Collvrewi.

91.   The three beneficial artisans of the Isle of Britain: Corvinwr the bard of Ceri of the long white lake, who first made a ship with sail and rudder for the Cambrian nation; Morddal the man of the white torrent, the artist of Ceraint son of Greidiawl, who first taught the Cambrians to work with stone and lime (at the time the emperor Alexander was subduing the world); and Coel son of Cyllin, grandson of Caradog, and great grandson of Bran, who first made a mill of round and wheel for the Cambrians; and these three were bards.

92.   The three inventors of song and record of the Cambrian nation: Gwyddon Ganhebon, who was the first in the world that composed vocal song; Hu the Mighty, who first applied vocal song to strengthen memory and record; and Tydain the father of poetic genius, who first conferred art on poetic song and made it the medium of record. From what was done by these three men, originated bards and bardism, and the privilege and institutes of these things were organised by the three primary bards, Plennydd, Alawn, and Gwron.

93.   The three primary youth-trainers of the Isle of Britain: Tydain the father of poetic genius; Menw the Aged; and Gwrhir bard of Teilaw in Llandav; and these three were bards.

94.   The three monster bulls of the Isle of Britain: the monster of Gwidawl; the monster of Llyr Merini; and the monster of Gwrthmwl Wledig.

95.   The three wild monsters of the Isle of Britain: the monster of Bannawg; the monster of Melan; and the monster of Ednyvedawg Drythyll.

96.   The three viragoes of the Isle of Britain: Llewei daughter of Seithwedd Saidi; Mederai daughter of Padellvawr; and Rhorei the Great, daughter of Usber Galed.

97.   The three primary and extraordinary works
of the Isle of Britain: the ship of Nwydd Nav
Neivion, which brought in it a male and female of
all living things when the lake of floods burst forth;
the large horned oxen of Hu the Mighty, that drew
the crocodile from the lake to the land, so that the
lake did not burst forth any more; and the stone of
Gwyddon Ganhebon, upon which all the arts and
sciences in the world are engraven.

98.   The three happy youth-trainers of the Isle of
Britain: Catwg son of Gwynlliw in Llangarvan;
Madawg Morvryn in the choir of Illtyd; and Deiniol
Wyn in North Wales. These three were bards.

99.   The three shepherds of the tribes of the Isle
of Britain: Colwyn the shepherd of the tribe of
Bran, son of Llyr Llediaith, in Glamorgan; Pybydd
the Bald, shepherd of the tribe of Tegerin of the
family of Llwydiarth in Anglesea; and Gwessin the
shepherd of the tribe of Goronwy son of Ednywain
king of Tegeingl in Rhyvoniog, and his name was
called Gwesyn because he tended sheep. The num-
ber tended by each of these three men was 120,000,
and each had under him three hundred slaves in the
protection of the Cambrian nation.

100.   The three men who exposed themselves and
their progeny to disgrace and loss of privilege, so
that they could never recover any rank but that of
bondmen. The first was Mandubratius son of Lludd,
who first invited the Romans to this Island with the
army of Julius Caesar their commander, and who
gave them land in the Isle of Thanet. The second
was Vortigern, who first invited the Saxons to this
Island that they might support him in his tyranny,
and he gave them land in the Isle of Thanet, and
misery came upon him for giving landed property
in this Island to strangers. He married Rowena the
daughter of Horsa, and the son he obtained by
marriage he called Gotta; and he gave him the
usurped rank of the monarchy of the Isle of Britain.
On this account the Cambrians lost the monarchy
of the Isle of Britain. The third was Medrawd son
of Llew, son of Cynvarch, who obtained the sover-
eignty of the Isle of Britain in trust, while Arthur
fought the Romans beyond the Alps, because they
wished to invade this Island again; and there Arthur
lost the flower of his troops. When Medrawd heard
of the circumstance, he united with the Saxons, and
caused the battle of Camlan, where Arthur and all
his men were slain, three excepted. Upon this, the
Saxons violently usurped the sovereignty of the Isle
of Britain, and murdered and cruelly used every
person of the Cambrian nation who would not join
them; and all those of the nation who desired to
oppose the Saxon invasions, obtained only the
country of Cambria. The Romans also confirmed
the privilege and the lands to the Saxons, as if the
invading nation were forming a close alliance with
the other, until the Romans were visited in such a
manner, that envy burnt their possessions and the
black intrusion came upon themselves.

101.   The three powerful swineherds of the Isle of
Britain. The first was Pryderi son of Pwyll Pendaran
of Dyved, who kept his father's swine whilst he was
yet in Annwn; and he kept them in the vale of
Cwch in Emlyn. The second was Coll son of
Collvrewi, who kept the sow of Dallwaran Dalben
that came burrowing as far as Penrhyn Penwedig in
Cornwall; and then going on the sea, she came to
land at Aber Tarogi in Gwent Iscoed. And Coll son
of Collvrewi kept his hand in her bristles wherever
she went, whether by land or sea. And in Maes
Gwenith, in Gwent, she deposited three grains of
wheat and three bees; and on that account the best
wheat and honey are in Gwent. From Gwent she
proceeded to Dyved and deposited a grain of barley
and a little pig at Llonio Llonwen; and on this
account the best barley and swine are reared in
Dyved. After this she proceeded to Arvon, and
deposited a grain of rye in Lleyn; and therefore
the best rye is raised in Lleyn and Eivionydd. Upon
the skirt of Rhiwgyverthwch she deposited a wolf's
cub and a young eaglet, and Coll gave the eagle to
Brynach the Irishman, and he gave the wolf to
Menwaed lord of Arllechwedd; and was there much
talk about the wolf of Brynach and the eagle of
Menwaed. From there she went to Maen Du in
Arvon where she deposited a kitten, and Coll son
of Collvrewi threw it into the Menai; and this was
the glossy smooth cat that became a molestation
to the Isle of Anglesea. The third was Trystan son
of Tallwch who kept the swine of March son of
Meirchion, whilst the swineherd went on a message
to Essyllt to desire an interview with her. And
Arthur, Marchell, Cai, and Bedwyr were the four
who looked for an opportunity, but they could not
obtain as much as one pig either by gift, purchase,

deceit, violence or theft. They were, therefore, called the three powerful swineherds, because it was not possible to gain or prevail over them for one swine which they kept; for they restored them with their full increase to their owners.

102.   The three amorous ones of the Isle of Britain. The first was Caswallawn son of Beli, for Flur, daughter of Mygnach the Dwarf, and he went for her as far as the land of Gascony against the Romans, and he brought her away, and killed 6,000 Caesarians; and in revenge the Romans invaded this Island. The second was Trystan son of Tallwch, for Essyllt daughter of March son of Meirchion his uncle. The third was Cynon, for Morvydd daughter of Urien Rheged.

103.   The three chaste maids of the Isle of Britain: Trywyl daughter of Llynghesawl with the generous hand; Gwenvron daughter of Tudwal Tudclud; and Tegau Eurvron, who was one of the three beauteous dames in the court of Arthur.

104.   The three chaste wives of the Isle of Britain: Arddun wife of Catgor and son of Collwyn; Eviliau wife of Gwydyr Trwm; and Emerched wife of Mabon and son of Dewain the Aged.

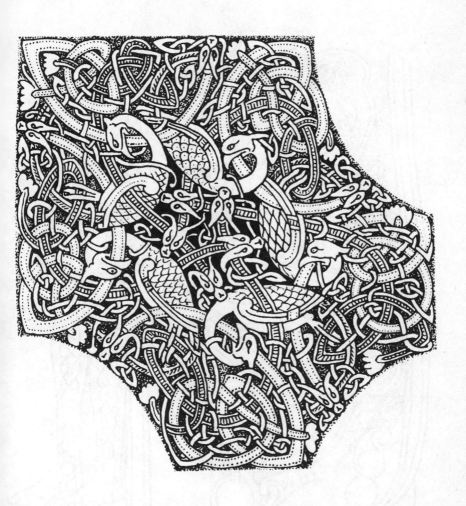

105. The three unchaste wives of the Isle of
Britain were the three daughters of Culvynawyd
Prydain: the first was Essyllt Vyngwen the mistress
of Trystan son of Tallwch; the second was
Penarwen wife of Owain son of Urien; and the
third was Bun wife of Ida the flame-bearer.

106. The three sprightly maids of the Isle of
Britain: Anghared Tonvelen daughter of Rhydderch
the Generous; Anan daughter of Maig Mygedwas;
and Perwyr daughter of Rhun Ryseddvawr.

107. The three beautiful maids of the Isle of
Britain: Gwen daughter of Cywryd son of Crydon;
Creirwy daughter of Ceridwen; and Arianrod
daughter of Dôn.

108. The three beautiful ladies of the court of
Arthur: Dyvir with the golden coloured hair; Enid
daughter of Yniwl, the earl; and Tegau Eurvron.
These were the three excellent ladies of Arthur's
court.

109. The three wives of Arthur, who were his
three chief ladies: that is to say, Gwenhwyvar
daughter of Gwythyr and son of Greidiawl;
Gwenhwyvar daughter of Gawrwyd Ceint; and
Gwenhwyvar daughter of Ogyrvan Gawr.

110. The three chief mistresses of Arthur: the
first was Garwen daughter of Henyn of Tegyrn
Gwyr and Ystrad Tywy; Gwyl daughter of Eutaw
of Caerworgorn; and Indeg daughter of Avarwy the
Tall of Radnorshire.

111.   The three chief courts of Arthur: Caerllion
upon Usk in Cambria; Celliwig in Cornwall; and
Edinburgh in the North. These are the three at
which he kept the three chief festivals; that is to
say, Christmas, Easter and Whitsuntide.

112.   The three free guests having origin in the
court of Arthur: Llywarch Hen son of Elidir
Lydanwyn; Lemonening; and Heiddyn the Tall;
and these three were bards.

113.   The three compeers of the court of Arthur:
Dalldav son of Cynin Cov; Trystan son of March
son of Meirchion; and Rhyhawd son of Morgant
son of Adras.

114.   The three princes of the court of Arthur;
Goronwy son of Echel of Vorddwydtwll; Cadraith
son of Porthor Godo; Vleidur Vlam son of Godo.
That is to say, they were princes possessing
territory and dominion, but notwithstanding this,
they preferred remaining as knights in Arthur's
court, judging that to be superior to all honour and
dignity; and they went by the name of the three
just knights.

115.   The three golden-tongued knights of
Arthur's court: Gwalchmai son of Gwyar; Drudwas
son of Tryphin; and Eliwlod son of Madog son of
Uthur. They were the wisest of all the wise of their
time; and so fair and gentlemanly was their deport-
ment, and so mellifluous and eloquent in all their
addresses, that no one could refuse to grant them
what they desired.

116.   The three wise counselling knights of
Arthur's court: Cynon son of Clydno Eiddin;
Arawn son of Cynvarch; and Llywarch Hen son of
Elidir Lydanwyn. Prosperity always followed their
counsels, if they were attended to, and misfortune
happened wherever their counsels were neglected.

117.   The three just dispensing knights of
Arthur's court: Blas son of the prince of Llychlyn;
Cadawg son of Gwynlliw the warrior; and Padrogyl
the spear-splinterer, son of the king of India. The
dispositions of these were to defend all feeble ones,
orphans, widows, virgins, and all who had placed
themselves under the protection of God and his
tranquillity, and all the poor and weak, without
exception, and to save them from violence, injury
and oppression:— Blas by the common law;
Padrogyl by the law of arms; and Cadawg by the
law of the church and the ordinances of God. And
they acted neither from respect, nor fear, nor
from love, nor hatred, nor from passion, nor from
complaisance, nor from anger, nor from mercy of
any kind, but only because it was just and right,
according to the law of God, the nature of good-
ness, and the demands of justice.

118.   The three kingly knights of Arthur's court:
Morgan the Greatly Courteous son of Adras;
Medrawd son of Llew son of Cynvarch; and Howel
son of Emyr of Armorica. It was their disposition
to be so placid, and mild, and pure in their dis-
course, that it was difficult for any person to refuse
what they wanted.

119.   The three lovely knights of Arthur's court:
the best towards every guest and stranger:
Gwalchmai son of Gwyar; Garwy son of Geraint
son of Erbin; and Cadeir the adopted son of Seithin
Saidai. And no one could be denied what he sought
from their courtesy, and so great was their generos-
ity towards every person, that what they gained
was the same as if a friend had obtained it on
account of real friendship.

120.   The three privileged knights of Arthur's
court: Eithew son of Gwrgawn; Colledawg son of
Gwyn; and Geraint the Tall son of Cymmanon the
Aged. They were plebeians, and the sons of vassals:
but their word and their disposition for honesty,
urbanity, gentleness, wisdom, bravery, justice,
mercy, and every praiseworthy quality and science,
either in peace, or in war, were so good, that the
court of Arthur and its privileges were free for
them.

121.   The three knights of Arthur's court who
guarded the Greal: Cadawg son of Gwynlliw; Illtud
the sainted knight; and Peredur son of Evrawg.

122.   The three continual knights of Arthur's
court: Cadawg son of Gwynlliw; Illtud the knight;
and Bwrt son of Bwrt king of Llychlyn. That is,
not one of them would commit a carnal sin, nor
would they form any matrimonial connection, nor
have any connections with women, but chose to
live as bachelors and to conduct themselves by the
law of God and the Christian faith.

123.   The three vain bards of the Isle of Britain:
the first was Arthur; the second was Cadwallawn
son of Cadvan; and the third was Rhyhawd the
adopted son of Morgant of Glamorgan.

124.   The three golden shoe-wearers of the Isle of
Britain. Caswallawn son of Beli, when he went into
Gascony to obtain Flur the daughter of Mygnach
the Dwarf, who had been taken there clandestinely
to the emperor Caesar by a person called Mwrchan
the Thief, king of that country, and the friend of
Julius Caesar; and Caswallawn brought her back
again to the Isle of Britain. Second, Manawydan
son of Llyr Llediaith, when he went as far as Dyved
imposing restrictions. Third, Llew Llaw Gyfes,
when he went with Gwydion son of Dôn, seeking
a name and purpose of Riannon his mother.

125.   The three chief Christian bards of the Isle of
Britain: Merddin bard of Ambrosius; Taliesin
chief of the bards; and Merddin son of Madawg
Morvryn.

126.   The three royal domains which were estab-
lished by Rhodri the Great in Cambria: the first is
Dinevor; the second Aberfraw; and the third
Mathravael. In each of these three domains there
is a prince wearing a diadem; and the oldest of these
three princes, whichever of them it might be, is to
be sovereign; that is, king of all Cambria. The other
two must be obedient to his commands, and his
command is imperative upon each of them. He is
also chief of law and of eldership in every collective
convention and in every movement of the country
and the tribe.

George Bain.

GLOSSARY

The Glossary provides a brief indication of the historical or legendary character of the places and persons mentioned therein. Those who want more detailed information are referred to the Bibliography on page 112.

ABER TAROGI IN GWENT ISCOED, 101: In the southern division of Gwent, lying alongside the Bristol Channel south of Wentwood.
ABERFRAW, 43,126: Sometime capital of the kings of Gwynedd, on the coast of Anglesey (Môn).
AEDD THE GREAT, 1-4,34,36,54,55,59: Father of Prydain. The name occurs frequently in Irish legend, but no material concerning the British Aedd has survived.
AEDDAN, THE TRAITOR OF THE NORTH, 45,52,80: Aeddan Vradawc (='the Wily'), identified as Aedan mac Gabrain, the Irish ruler of the kingdom of Dal Riada in Argyllshire, c.573-608 A.D. In 603 A.D. he led an army against the Saxon king, Ethelfrith, and was defeated at Degsastan. If this battle can be equated with Cattraeth, then the army commanded by Aeddan was partly British and the defeat may have earned him his epithet.
ALAN MORGAN, 81: Alan Fyrgan, Duke of

Brittany, d. 1119 A.D. His inclusion in this Triad
may be a late substitution, or carry a satirical or
political intention.

ALAWN, PRIMARY BARD, 58,92.

ALIS RONWEN, 21: Daughter of Hengist or Horsa,
second wife of Vortigern. According to Geoffrey
of Monmouth she poisoned her step-son Gwrthevyr
(Vortimer) after he assumed the kingship from his
father Vortigern.

AMBROSIUS, 34,53,84: Ambrosius Aurelianus, a
battle-leader of the Britons, active c.460-475 A.D.
A genuine historical figure, perhaps of Roman des-
cent, many legends have attached to his name. He
is identified with the Welsh 'Emrys'.

ANAN, DAUGHTER OF MAIG MYGEDWAS, 106.

ANARAWD, KING OF ABERFRAW, 43: King of
Gwynedd, c.877-915 A.D. Son of Rhodri the Great.

ANEURIN, 47,48: A sixth century bard whose
poem 'Y Gododdin' celebrates the British heroes
who fell at the battle of Cattraeth, c.600 A.D.

ANGHARED TONVELEN, 106: Literally,
Anghared 'Yellow Wave', i.e., 'Yellow Tresses'.

ANNWN, 101: Annwfn, the Celtic Otherworld.

ARAVIA, 21: Arabia.

ARAWN, SON OF CYNVARCH, 116: Legendary
brother of Urien Rheged who ruled the northern-
most kingdom of the Britons, Prydyn, in the time
of King Arthur. Arawn is also the name given to
the king of the Celtic Otherworld, Annwfn, who
fought against Gwydion at the battle of Goddeu,
q.v.

ARDDUN, WIFE OF CATGOR, 104: Possibly a
sister of Gwrgi and Peredur, q.v.

ARDERYDD, 50,79: A renowned battle, fought in
573 A.D. at Arthuret near Carlisle, in which
Gwenddoleu was killed fighting Gwrgi and Peredur.

The cause may have been connected with a border dispute, and the 'bird's nest' perhaps refers to Caerlaverock (Larkfort) near the scene of the battle.

ARDUDWY, 37,81: Coastal province near Harlech.

ARIANROD, 14,107: Daughter of Beli and Dôn, sister of Gwydion, mother of Llew Llaw Gyfes. Literally, 'Silver Wheel'. Her story is found in 'Math, Son of Mathonwy' (Mabinogion).

ARMORICA, 4,5,14: Brittany.

ARTHUR, 20-23,29,31,45,50-53,64,70,100,101, 103,108-123: A battle-leader (not a king) of the fifth century Britons, active c.475-515 A.D. He appears to have won several important victories over Saxon adversaries and thus stemmed the advance of the invaders for half a century. Many legends attach to his name, and the cultus of Arthur was greatly enhanced in the twelfth century by Geoffrey of Monmouth's History and subsequent Arthurian romances.

ARVON, 37: Cantref and province in the region of Bangor, North Wales.

AVAN VERDDIG, 40: Literally, Avan 'the little bard'.

AVAON, 47,73,76: Son of Taliesin, included in 'The Dream of Rhonabwy' (Mabinogion).

BALD MAN, 82: Probably St. Augustine, reputed to have said, 'If the Welsh (i.e., the Welsh clergy) will not have peace with us, they shall perish at the hands of the Saxons.' The 'prophecy' was realised in 607 A.D., near Chester, when Ethelfrith's army slew a contingent of Welsh priests from Bangor.

BEDWINI, 64: Bishop at Celliwig. Bedwini is named in a number of Arthurian stories.

BEDWYR, SON OF PEDRAWG, 69,101: One of the earliest companions of Arthur, better known as Sir Bedevere.

BELI, SON OF MYNOGAN, 8,11,14,17,21,24,31,
53,124: An 'illustrious ancestor' of the genealogies,
of whom little is known. Geoffrey of Monmouth
features him twice in his History; once as the
conqueror-King Belinus, and then as Hely, the
father of Lud (Lludd), Cassibelaunus (Caswallawn)
and Nennius. Beli has been compared with the Irish
deity, Bile.
BELYN, SON OF CYNVELYN, 79: Possibly
Belinus, or Beli (above), son of Cunobelinus.
BELYN OF LLEYN, 27: Perhaps an ally of
Cadwallon in the struggle against Edwin of North-
umbria. The peninsula of Lleyn lies south of
Anglesey in Gwynedd.
BENREN, HERDSMAN IN GORWENNYDD, 85.
BLAS, SON OF THE PRINCE OF LLYCHLYN,
117: The hermit, Blase, who recorded Merlin's
prophecies and wrote the early history of the Grail
may derive from Blas. Llychlyn generally denotes
Scandinavia.
BOADICEA, 18,22,35: Queen of the tribe of Iceni,
who led a rebellion against the Roman power, and
died by suicide c.61 A.D. Cartismandu, queen of
the Brigantes, was the actual betrayer of Caradog.
BOULOGNESE, 14: Unmentioned by variant
Triads.
BRAN, SON OF LLYR LLEDIAITH, 17,18,22-24,
34-36,38,41,53,55,91,99: Brother of Bronwen and
Manawydan. Literally, 'Raven'. A presumed god of
the ancient Britons, his precise functions are now
obscure.. He appears, in giant form, in the story of
'Branwen' (Mabinogion) where he is fatally wounded
and decapitated at his own request. The 'wonderful
head' lives on until it is buried in London to protect
Britain from invasion. Bran Bendegeit ('the Blessed'),

passed into Christian lore at St. Bran, and into the Arthurian cycles as Sir Brons and King Ban of Benwick.

BRONWEN, DAUGHTER OF LLYR LLEDIAITH, 49: The sister of Bran, also known as Branwen. Literally, 'White Breast' or 'White Raven'. Her ill-treatment at the hands of King Matholwch of Ireland led to the wars in which Bran received his fatal wound. Bronwen returned to Wales but died there of a broken heart.

BRYCHAN OF BRECKNOCKSHIRE, 18: Eponymous founder recorded by Giraldus Cambrensis as 'Brachanus...ruler of Brecheinoc'. Otherwise St. Brychan, father of several fifth — sixth century saints.

BRYNACH THE IRISHMAN, 101: Sometimes as 'Breat'.

BUN, WIFE OF IDA, 105: Literally, 'Maiden'.

BWRT, SON OF BWRT KING OF LLYCHLYN, 122: The Sir Bors or Bohort of Arthurian romance.

CADAVAEL, SON OF CYNVEDW, 26: Mid-seventh century king of Gwynedd, possibly a usurper, who seems to have performed badly in battle despite the commendations of this Triad.

CADAVAEL THE WILD, 48: Other sources indicate that Jago (Iago) died of natural causes or in battle, c.613 A.D. Cadavael may be a displaced memory of the son of Cynvedw (above), active c.655 A.D.

CADAWG, SON OF GWYNLLIW, 117,121,122: Sixth century abbot and reputed founder of a monastery at Llancarfan, near Cardiff. Better known as St. Cadoc.

CADEIR, 119: Literally, 'Fine Speech' (as Cadyreith, in variant spellings). 'Adopted son' can signify descendant.

CADELL, KING OF DINEVOR, 43,59: King of
Deheubarth (South Wales) after the death of
Rhodri Mawr.

CADRAITH, SON OF PORTHOR GODO, 114.

CADWALADYR THE BLESSED, 28,35,48,49:
Son of Cadwallon. Cadwaladyr's 'blessedness' arises
from a confusion with the Saxon king of Wessex,
Caedwalla, who made a pilgrimage to Rome and
died there in 669 A.D. Cadwaladyr's death is
variously given as 682 and 689 A.D.

CADWALLON, SON OF CADVAN, 40,80,122:
The great great grandson of Maelgwn, Cadwallon
was king of Gwynedd c.625-634 A.D. Forced into
exile by Edwin, the Saxon king of Northumbria,
Cadwallon later returned and triumphed over his
enemy in 633 A.D. He ravaged Northumbria until
his death in 634 A.D. at Denisesburn, earning the
censure of Bede and gaining a reputation among
the Britons as a 'deliverer' who would one day, like
Arthur, return.

CAI, SON OF CYNYR, 69,101: Like Bedwyr, an
early companion of Arthur and notable for several
supernatural attributes. He could endure fire and
water for lengthy periods, grow taller than a tree,
and carry a burden so that it would not be seen
from the front or behind. Always impetuous, he
was degraded in later writings to the buffoonish
Sir Kay of Arthur's court. An early legend credits
him as the murderer of Arthur's son, Llacheu
(Lohot).

CALEDONIANS, 6: The tribe of the Caledonii,
precursors of the historical Picts.

CAMBRIA, LLOEGRIA AND ALBAN, 1: Wales,
England and Scotland. According to Geoffrey of
Monmouth, the names derive from the three sons
of Brutus (see Prydain): Camber; Locrine and

Albanact. Lloegria is better known as Logres;
Alban as Albany.

CAMBRIANS, LLOEGRIANS AND BRYTHONS,
5: Archaeological evidence reveals three main occu-
pations of Britain by Celtic tribes: the Hallstadt
Celts (600-500 B.C.), the La Tene Celts (c.250 B.C.),
and the iron-working Belgae (c.100 B.C.).

CAMLAN, 49-51,81,83,100: The famous battle in
which Arthur and Mordred (see Medrawd) fell. The
precise location remains unknown but it is likely
to have been in the north, not the south-west where
it is traditionally located.

CARADOG, SON OF BRAN, 17,22,23,34,35,41,
55,79,85,91: Also as Caradawc, Caradawg. In the
story of 'Branwen' (Mabinogion), he is left with six
companions as overseer of Britain during Bran's
absence in Ireland, and, when these are murdered
through the deceit of Caswallawn, Caradog dies of
a broken heart. Later commentators identify
Caradog with the historical Caratacus, a chieftain
of the Silures who spent part of his life as a captive
in Rome.

CARADOG WITH THE BRAWNY ARM, 29,41,
64: Caradawc Vreiehvras, son of Llyr Merini.
Possibly cognate with Caradog (above). He enters
Arthurian romance as King Carados.

CARNOBAN, 7: In the commot of Deira and
Bernicia.

CASWALLAWN WITH THE LONG HAND, 27:
Grandson of Cynedda Wledig, Caswallawn Law Hir
completed the expulsion of Irish settlers from
Gwynedd, c.525 A.D. The Caswallawn of Triad 8,
given as 'son of Beli' refers to Caswallawn Law Hir.

CASWALLON, SON OF BELI, 8,14,17,24,102,
124: Cassivelaunus, historically a leader of the tribe
of Catuvellauni who opposed Julius Caesar in 54

B.C. In legend, the brother of Lludd, Llefelys, Penardun (wife of Llyr), Nynnyaw and Peibaw, who usurped the kingdom of Britain and dispossessed the heirs of Llyr. In Geoffrey of Monmouth, similarly, he assumes the crown on the death of his brother King Lud, dispossessing his nephews, Androgeus and Tenuantius.

CAT, GLOSSY SMOOTH, 101: The Cat Palug or Paluc's Cat.

CATTRAETH, 79: Identified with Catterick, Yorkshire. Site of a disastrous battle, c.600 A.D., in which many British warriors and chieftains fell in combat with the Saxons. Almost certainly Cattraeth can be equated with Degsastan (see Aeddan), 603 A.D.

CATWG, SON OF GWYNLLIW, 98: See Cadawg.

CAWRDAV, 41: Son of Caradog with the Brawny Arm. Given, in one genealogy, as the father of Iddawg Corn Prydain. One of Arthur's counsellors in 'The Dream of Rhonabwy' (Mabinogion).

CEIDIAW, FATHER OF GWENDDOLEU, 46,72, 80.

CERAINT, DRUNKEN KING OF SILURIA, 37.

CETI, STONE OF, 88: 'Maen Cetti' or 'Arthur's Stone', a Megalithic chamber on the Gower Peninsula at Reynoldstone, with a capstone weighing twenty-five tons.

CEUGANT BEILLIAWG, 77: Cengan Peilliavc in other versions of this Triad.

COEL, SON OF CYLLIN, 35,62,91: Founder of several northern dynasties, claimed as the ancestor of Urien Rheged, Llywarch Hen, Gwenddoleu, Peredur and others. The probable source of 'Old King Cole' who still preserves a triad of fiddlers in his rhyme.

COLEDDAWG, SON OF GWYN, 120.

COLL, SON OF COLLVREWI, 56,90,101: In a
variant of Triad 90, Coll himself is hailed as one of
three great enchanters of the Isle of Britain.

COLWYN, SHEPHERD OF BRAN, 99.

CONSTANTINE, 62: Constantine I, Emperor of
Rome, 312-337 A.D. The first Christian Emperor.

CONSTANTINE THE BLESSED, 21,44: Custennin
Vendigeit. Constantine III, elected Emperor of
Rome by troops in Britain, 407 A.D. He was execu-
ted four years after his election by Honorius, after
he had fled for sanctuary in Arles and taken holy
orders.

CORANIANS, 7,14,15: Deriving either from the
tribe of the Coritanii, or the old Welsh word 'Cor'
(='dwarf'). The Coranians feature in the story of
'Lludd and Llefelys' (Mabinogion) as one of three
plagues which afflict Lludd's kingdom.

CORVINWR, BARD OF CERI, 91.

CRAU, FORTRESS OF, 81.

CREIRWY, 107: The daughter of Ceridwen and
Tegid Voel. Her brother, Affagdu (see Morvran),
was the ugliest boy; Creirwy, the most beautiful
girl.

CROCODILE, 1: Probably the Afanc, a lake-dwelling
monster similar to the Scottish 'kelpie' or 'water-
horse'. In modern Welsh, Afanc = beaver.

CULVYNAWD PRYDAIN, 105.

CUNOBELINUS, 23,24: A ruler of the Catuvellauni,
perhaps the great grandson of Cassivellaunus (see
Caswallon). The Welsh form of Cunobelinus is
Cynvelyn; the English (via Shakespeare), Cymbeline.

CWCH IN EMLYN, 101: The river Cuch in the
region between Cardigan and Newcastle Emlyn.

CYNAN, LORD OF MEIRIADOG, 14: Brother of
Elen Bellipotent, who settled in Brittany after the
legendary conquest of Rome. Like Arthur and

Cadwallon, a military hero of the Britons expected
to return.
CYNDEYRN GARTHWYS, 64: St. Kentigern,
patron saint of Glasgow.
CYNEDDA WLEDIG, 18,64: Ruler of the Votadini
who led his people into Gwynedd (North Wales),
c.400 A.D., to expel the Irish who had settled there.
A dynastic founder whose descendants include
Caswallawn Law Hir, St. David, Maelgwn, Rhun and
Cadwallon. The epithet 'Wledig' denotes 'ruler' or
'lord'.
CYNHAVAL, SON OF ARGAD, 73.
CYNON, SON OF CLYDNO EIDDIN, 102,116:
A hero of the northern Britons and lover of
Morvydd, daughter of Urien of Rheged.
CYNVAR CADGADAWG, 72: A northern ruler,
and perhaps the great great grandfather of Cynon.
CYNVARCH, 21,47,100,118: A descendant of
Coel, and father of Urien of Rheged.
CYNVELYN THE STUMBLER, 71: Cynvelyn
Drwsgyl, descendant of Coel and hero of the north
Britons.
CYVRANGON, PILE OF, 88.
DALLDAV, SON OF CYNIN COV, 113.
DALLWAREN DALBEN, SOW OF, 101: In a
variant Triad the sow is named Henwen (='the old
white one'). Although Celtic tradition associates
the colour white with the Otherworld, the signifi-
cance of the Triad is now obscure. The journey may
provide a *raison d'être* for the place names men-
tioned on the way, whilst comparing South Wales
favourably with the North.
DEFROBANI, 4,54: The Summer Country, located
in the region of Constantinople by Probert. Robert
Graves, in 'The White Goddess', gives Ceylon.

DEINIOL WYN, 98: Sixth century abbot-bishop who is credited with founding colleges in Bangor Fawr and Bangor Iscoed. Perhaps the son of Dunawd Fur.

DEIRA AND BERNICIA, 7,39,66,75,87: Territories settled by the Saxons in the sixth century. Deira was roughly comprised of the East Riding of Yorkshire; Bernicia, to the north, centred around Bamburgh in Northumberland. With the Saxon advance they later combined into the kingdom of Northumbria.

DIFIDEL, 39,46: See Gall.

DIMETIA, 37: That part of Wales once occupied by the Demetae. The name survives, in altered form, as Dyved.

DINEVOR, 43,126: Capital of Cadell, king of South Wales, situated west of Llandeilo Fawr in Dyfed.

DIVWG, SON OF ALBAN, 86.

DOLOR, SON OF MWRCHATH KING OF MANAW, 86: Manaw was the name given to the Isle of Man.

DRUDWAS, SON OF TRYPHIN, 115: In legend, the son of the king of Denmark mistakenly killed by his own 'griffins' while fighting in single combat with Arthur.

DRYWON, SON OF NUDD THE GENEROUS, 79.

DUNAWD FUR, SON OF PABO, 71: A northern chieftain, active in the late sixth century, who appears to have fought against Urien's sons Owain and Pasgen.

DWYVAN AND DWYVACH, 13: Interpreted as 'the god' and 'the goddess', the two survivors of the Deluge. According to one account, the Flood was caused when the Afanc (see Crocodile) overflowed

Llyon Llion, the Lake of Floods. Dwyvan and
Dwyvach escaped in the ship built by Nefyed Nav
Nevion.

DYGYNNELW, BARD OF OWAIN, 40.

DYVIR WITH THE GOLDEN HAIR, 108.

DYVNWAL MOELMUD, 4,11,36,57,59: Dyvnwal
Moelmud appears in Geoffrey's History as
Dunwallo Molmutius, a Cornish noble who defeats
the three kings of Cambria, Lloegria and Alban to
become the sole king of Britain. During his reign
he issues the Molmutine Laws which, among others,
grant the right of sanctuary in temples and cities,
and the right of protection on highways. A collec-
tion of nearly 250 legal triads, said to be those of
Dyvnwal Moelmud, is still extant.

EDELFLED, THE SAXON KING, 45,46:
Ethelfrith, the grandson (?) of Ida, king of Bernicia
593-617 A.D. Unless Ysgavnell is somehow cognate
with Redwald the account of his death in the Triads
is wishful thinking. He was killed by the latter, a
king of the East Angles, in 617 A.D.

EDINBURGH, 64: The Triads name Pen Rhionydd,
an unidentified location in the north, and not
Edinburgh.

EIDDILIC THE DWARF, 50,78,90.

EIDDIN, SON OF EINYGAN, 47,48: The name,
Eiddin, derives from the region whose name is re-
tained in Edinburgh.

EIDIOL THE MIGHTY, 60: Eidiol appears in
Geoffrey of Monmouth's History as Eldol, Duke of
Gloucester, who escaped the plot of Stonehenge,
joined forces with Ambrosius, and later had the
satisfaction of executing Hengist after the battle of
Knaresborough.

EITHEW, SON OF GWRGAWN, 120: Also as
Uchei.

ELEN BELLIPOTENT, 14: Elen Llwyddawc (='the Leader of Hosts'). Elen features as the wife of the Roman Emperor Macsen (Maximus) in the story 'The Dream of Macsen Wledic' (Mabinogion), who renders her husband good service by conquering Rome for him. She is often confused with Helena, the mother of Constantine I, who led a great army in search of Christ's cross, and Elen's epithet is perhaps owed to this mistake. She also appears, in other legends, as the wife of Merlin and founder of Caerfyrddin (Carmarthen), and enters the Arthurian romances as Elaine.

ELIWLOD, SON OF MADOG, 115: A nephew of Arthur who, on one occasion, took the form of an eagle.

ELLDUD, 56: St. Illtyd, fifth – sixth century saint of South Wales who is credited with a military career in the retinue of King Arthur before his calling to the religious life.

ELMUR, ADOPTED SON OF CIBDDAR, 73.

ELYSTAN GLODRYDD, 42: The allusion to 'fetters' is obscure; perhaps some token of fealty is implied to the rulers of Deheubarth, Powys and Gwynedd.

EMERCHED, WIFE OF MABON, 104.

EMRYS, 11: See Ambrosius.

ENID, DAUGHTER OF YNIWL, 108: Her story can be found in 'Gereint, Son of Erbin' (Mabinogion).

ENVAEL, SON OF ADRAN, 32.

ERIN, THE BELLIPOTENT OF SCANDINAVIA, 14.

ESSYLLT, 101,102: Better known as Iseult or Isolde, the wife (not daughter, as in Triad 102) of King Mark of Cornwall and the mistress of Sir Trystan.

ESSYLLT VYNGWEN, 105: Essyllt of the Fine Hair.

EVILIAU, WIFE OF GWYDYR TRWM, 104.

FLUR, DAUGHTER OF MYGNACH, 102,124: Julius Caesar and Caswallawn are both claimed as lovers of Flur. One account says Caswallawn left Britain to regain her from Julius, whilst another suggests that Julius came to Britain to wrest her from Caswallawn.

GADIAL, SON OF ERIN THE BELLIPOTENT, 14.

GAIR, SON OF GEIRION, 61: Also known as Gweir or Gwair. His imprisonment seems to be a variation of the Mabon-Modron myth (see Madawg, son of Medron). In this case his father, Geirion, is conjectured to be derived from 'Tigernonos' (='the Great King'); his mother must therefore be 'Rigantona' (='the Great Queen', the prototype of Rhiannon). Taliesin's poem 'The Spoils of Annwn' hints that Arthur delivered Gair from his captivity.

GALAS AND AVENA, 14: Unidentified. 'Galatae' was the Greek term for the Celts, as found in Galatia, settled by Celtic tribes c.450-300 B.C.

GALEDIN, 6,14: Probert supposes this to be Holland, though Triad 14 speaks of 'the border declivity of Galedin and Siluria'.

GALL, DIFIDEL AND YSGAVNELL, 39,46: The three sons of Dysgyvedog remain unidentified, as also the 'two brown birds of Gwenddoleu'. Since 'Edelfled' was killed by Redwald, king of the East Angles, and the name Gall derives from 'foreigner', perhaps the three are a confused recollection of Saxons who fought in alliance with the British, or who aided the British cause through their own ambitions.

GALLIWIG, 52, or CELLIWIG, 62,64,111: Kelli Wic, Cornwall, variously identified with Callington,

Gweek Wood, Calliwith and the fort of Kelly in Egloshayle.

GANVAL THE IRISHMAN, 8: A leader of the Irish settlers in Gwynedd (North Wales), ousted by Cynedda Wledig and his descendants.

GARWEN, DAUGHTER OF HENYN, 110: 'Fair Leg'.

GARWY, SON OF GERAINT,119: Also known as Cadwy or Gadwy; a descendant of the Dumnonian rulers of the south-west peninsula, active in the late sixth and early seventh centuries.

GASCONY, 14,101.

GAULS, 14: From the Latin 'Galli'; Celts.

GAVRAN, 10,80: Given as the son of Aeddan, but more likely to have been his father. The Green Islands of the Floods are identified with the Cape Verde Islands by Probert. Variant Triads mention only 'the disappearance by loss'.

GERAINT, SON OF ERBIN, 68,119: In legend, a knight of Arthur's court, whose story may be found in 'Gereint, Son of Erbin' (Mabinogion). Historically, a sixth century ruler of one of the Dumnonian kingdoms of the south-west: Gerontius.

GERAINT THE TALL, 120: In variant Triads as Gerenhyr or Cerenhyr, which has come to be rendered as Gereint Hir (= 'the Tall').

GLEWLWYD WITH THE MIGHTY GRASP, 83: Appears in the story of 'Culhwch and Olwen' (Mabinogion) as the head porter (gate-keeper) of Arthur's court.

GODDEU, BATTLE OF, 50: The battle of the Trees, fought between Gwydion, son of Dôn, and Arawn, the king of Annwn. Gwydion was victorious when he guessed the name of Arawn's ally, Bran. For an interpretation of this conflict, see Robert Graves, 'The White Goddess'.

GOLYDDAN THE BARD, 48,49.

GORONWY, SON OF ECHEL VORDDWYDTWLL, 114.

GORONWY, SON OF EDNYWAIN, 99.

GORONWY THE FAIR, 81: The lover of Blodeuwedd, wife of Llew Llaw Gyfes. Llew killed him with a spear, despite the fact that Goronwy stood behind a stone to protect himself.

GORWENNYDD, 14,85.

GOTTA, SON OF VORTIGERN, 21,100: Pascentius is given by Geoffrey of Monmouth as the son of Vortigern who vied with Ambrosius for the crown. Hengist's son, Ochta, may be intended here.

GREIDIAWL, 32,91: Greidiawl Galovyd or Gallddofydd. 'Lord over foes' or 'conqueror of enemies' might be closer than 'resolute-minded ovate'.

GRUDNEW, HENBEN AND EIDNEW, 33: Sons of Hayarnwed the Treacherous (or Wily).

GWAELOD, 37: See Gwydnaw Garanhir.

GWAITHVOED, KING OF CARDIGAN, 42: Entered in some genealogies as a descendant of Gwydnaw Garanhir, and ancestor of Cynedda Wledig.

GWALCHMAI, SON OF GWYAR, 70,115,119: Literally, 'Falcon of May', the probable source of the Gawain of Arthurian romance.

GWALLAWG, SON OF LLEENAWG, 71,76: One of the heroes of the northern Britons; supposed ruler of the kingdom of Elmet, and part-enemy of Urien and his son, Owain.

GWANAR, SON OF LLIAWS, 14: See Gwenwynwyn.

GWEIRWERYDD THE GREAT, 78: Perhaps Gweir Gwrhyt Vawr, Gweir of Great Valour, who replaces

Envael in variants of Triad 32.

GWEIRYDD, SON OF CUNOBELINUS, 24: Given, by Geoffrey of Monmouth, as Guiderius, the British king who refused to pay tribute to the Emperor Claudius and thus precipitated the Roman invasion of Britain.

GWEN, DAUGHTER OF CYWRYD, 107: 'White'.

GWENDOLLEU, 46,72,80: Northern leader killed in the battle of Arderydd. Some references indicate that he was the patron of Merddin (Wyllt), and that his death was the cause of Merddin's madness. He owned one of the thirteen treasures of Britain: a game of gwyddbwyll (akin to chess) which would play by itself if the pieces were set out.

GWENHWYVACH, 49: The sister of Gwenhwyvar. The story of the 'fatal slap' is now lost.

GWENHWYVAR, 49,52,109: Wife of Arthur, better known as Guinevere. No account exists to explain the three Gwenhwyvars of Triad 109 but it is interesting to note that the cross 'discovered' with Arthur's grave at Glastonbury in the late twelfth century notes (according to one account of it) that he was buried with Guinevere (Wennerveria) 'his second wife'.

GWENTIANS, 16: From Gwent, south-east Wales.

GWENVRON, DAUGHTER OF TUDWAL TUDCLUD, 103: Literally, 'White Breast'.

GWENWYNWYN, SON OF LLIAWS, 14: Literally, 'White-white-white' or 'Thrice White One'. If, as has been proposed, Lliaws is a corruption of Nav, he is cognate with Gwenwynwyn (below).

GWENWYNWYN, SON OF NAV, 68: Mentioned in 'Culhwch and Olwen' (Mabinogion) as 'Arthur's first fighter'.

GWESSIN, SHEPHERD OF GORONWY, 99: Tegeingl is situated in Flintshire.

GWGAWN WITH THE MIGHTY HAND, 60.

GWGON THE HERO, 38: The grandson (not son) of Eleuver. The suggestion of Triad 38 is probably an attempt to put a good face on a *fait accompli*. Gwgon was almost certainly driven from his lands after the defeat of Gwrgi and Peredur at Caer Grau, 580 A.D.

GWIDAWL, 94: Perhaps related to Gwydelen Gor. See Rhuddlum the Giant.

GWRDDYLED OF THE CONFLICT, 44.

GWRGAI, SON OF GWRIEN, 26.

GWRGI, SON OF ELEUVER, 81: Brother of Peredur. Tradition maintains that he fought against Gwendolleu at Arderydd, and the 'Annales Cambriae' record his death in 580 A.D.

GWRGI GARWLWYD, 45,46,50: The name, according to Rachel Bromwich, can translate as 'Man-hound Rough-grey' and suggests affinities with a werewolf. He may be cognate with the cannibalistic giant of southern Welsh legend, Guurgint Barmh Truch, who supplied Geoffrey of Monmouth with the name of one of his legendary kings, Gurgiunt Brabtruc, and may also have provided the model for Rabelais' giant, Gargantua.

GWRHIR, 93: Saint and follower of St. Teilo (Teilaw).

GWRNERTH THE SHARP SHOT, 60.

GWRON, PRIMARY BARD, 58,92: Literally, 'Hero'.

GWRTHEVYR THE BLESSED, 53: Prince Vortimer of Geoffrey's History. The son of Vortigern by his first wife, he is credited with leading a number of successful attacks against the Saxons until his death, either in battle or at the hands of Alis Ronwen. Triad 53 states that his bones were disinterred: differing accounts maintain that they were not buried according to Gwrthevyr's wishes. His 'blessedness' is the result of a confusion with St. Gwrthiern.

GWRTHMWL WLEDIG, 64,94.

GWYDDNAW, 65: A legendary port in the drowned lands of Cantre'r Gwaelod. See Gwydnaw Garanhir.

GWYDDON GANHEBON, 92,97: Probably identical with Gwydion (below), who is described as 'the best teller of tales in the world' in the Mabinogion. Iolo Morganwg also records that Gwydion introduced the knowledge of letters into Wales.

GWYDION, SON OF DON, 85,89,90,124: A culture-hero of North Wales, well versed in the arts of magic. His story is found in 'Math, Son of Mathonwy' in the Mabinogion.

GWYDNAW GARANHIR, 37: Literally, Gwydnaw Long-Shanks, the ruler of Cantre'r Gwaelod (Bottom Cantref) which was inundated through the negligence of Seithynin. The origins of this legend reside in the petrified remains of primeval forests still visible in the shallows of Cardigan Bay. Gwydnaw owned one of the thirteen treasures of Britain: a hamper which would feed one hundred people if enough food for one was placed in it.

GWYL, DAUGHTER OF EUTAW, 110: Literally, 'Modest'.

GWYN, SON OF NUDD, 89: Literally, 'White'. In legend Gwyn was the abductor of Lludd's daughter, Creiddylad, the beloved of Gwythyr, son of Greidiawl. Arthur intervened in the ensuing feud, and adjudged that Creiddylad should return to Lludd whilst her two suitors engaged in battle each May-kalends until the day of doom. The victor at that point would win the maiden. Gwyn survived in later legend as the king of the fairies, and appears in Spenser's 'Faerie Queen' as Sir Guyon.

GWYR, 14: Gower and the adjacent parts of Glamorgan.

GWYTHYR, SON OF GREIDIAWL, 109: Literally, 'Victor, son of Scorcher'. See Gwyn (above).

HALF-APPARENT MAN, 11: Usually applied to shape-shifters or those with the power to make themselves invisible. If Lludd, the son of Beli, is substituted for Beli himself then the half-apparent man might be the third 'plague' afflicting Lludd's kingdom in the story of 'Lludd and Llefelys' (Mabinogion).

HAZY SEA, 4: The German Ocean.

HEIDDYN THE TALL, 112: Presumed an exile, like Llywarch Hen, seeking refuge in a friendly court.

HENGIST, 21,51,53: Brother of Horsa, father (?) of Alis Ronwen. Literally, 'Stallion'. In most accounts the leader of the Saxon mercenaries who arrived in Britain, c.430 A.D., at the behest of Vortigern to fight off the marauding Picts and Irish. In the 440s the Saxons turned on their hosts and so began the occupation of Britain which Ambrosius, Arthur and later British heroes strove unavailingly to avert.

HONEY ISLAND, 1: 'Y vel ynys', which Rachel Bromwich suggests is a corruption of 'Ynys Veli' or 'the Island of Beli'.

HORSA, 37,51,100: Brother of Hengist, father (?) of Alis Ronwen. Literally, 'Horse'. His death is given as 455 A.D. by the Anglo-Saxon Chronicle.

HOWEL, SON OF EMYR, 118: Legendary prince of Brittany and nephew of Arthur. Emyr denotes 'Ruler'.

HOWEL, THE GOOD, 59: The grandson of Rhodri

Mawr, who made submission to the Saxon king, Aethelstan, in 926 A.D. and briefly united Wales under his rule in 942 A.D.

HU THE MIGHTY, 4,5,54,56,57,92,97: Hu Gadarn, an early culture hero of the Welsh. The 'Pelerinage Charlemagne' includes an Emperor of Constantinople, Hugo, who makes use of a golden plough. In Welsh translations of the 'Pelerinage' Hugo was rendered as Hu Gadarn.

HUAIL, SON OF CAW, 69: An adversary of Arthur, who stabbed the king's nephew Gwydre and conducted raids on the kingdom during his short and stormy career. Two accounts say that Arthur killed him.

HYVAIDD THE TALL, 26: Son of St. Bleiddan, and one of the six companions of Caradog, son of Bran, who were murdered by the usurper Caswallawn. Bleiddan is identified with St. Lupus (both names designating 'wolf'), the companion of St. Germanus during his visit to Britain early in the fifth century.

IDA THE FLAME-BEARER, 105: A descendant of Ida of Bernicia (c.547-560 A.D.) known to the Britons by the nickname Fflamdwyn. The identification with Ida is a late interpolation.

IDA THE GREAT KNEE, 81: Ida Glinvawr, recorded by Nennius as the great great grandson of Ida, king of Bernicia, and thus impossibly late for the victory over Gwrgi and Peredur. Ida's son, Eadric, seems the better candidate.

IDDAWG CORN PRYDAIN, 20,22: Literally, Iddawg 'the Embroiler of Britain'. Iddawg earned his epithet by his actions before Camlan when, sent to Mordred by Arthur with 'reasonable terms' to avert the battle, he presented them in such a way as to inflame Mordred and so provoke the conflict.

IDRIS THE GIANT, 89: Cadair Idris, the 'chair' of Idris, is located near Dolgellau in West Wales. Whoever spends the night there will be found, next day, either inspired or insane.

ILLTUD or ILLTYD, 98,121,122: See Elldud (above).

INDEG, DAUGHTER OF AVARWY THE TALL, 110.

IRISH, 6,7,9,14,53,61: The Gwyddyl. A better term might be 'Gaels', i.e., a racial or linguistic definition, rather than a geographical one.

JAGO, SON OF BELI, 48: An early seventh century king of Gwynedd. His father is not the Beli (above), but a descendant of Maelgwn.

JULIUS CAESAR, 21,51,100,124: Other accounts say that Julius gained his foot-hold on Thanet through the gift of a horse, Meinlas, to Caswallawn.

LAKE OF FLOODS, 13: See Dwyvan and Dwyvach.

LEMONENING, 112: A related form of this name, (Llwch) Lleminawc, has been conjectured as the source of Lancelot du Lac.

LLAN ILLTYD VAWR, 84: Named after St. Illtyd, and anglicised as Llantwit Major, Glamorganshire.

LLANDAV, 35,62,93: Episcopal see near Cardiff.

LLAWGAD TRWM BARGAWD, 47.

LLAWR, SON OF EIDRIV, 86.

LLAWVRODEDD THE KNIGHT, 85: His knife was one of the thirteen treasures of Britain, able to serve for twenty four men sitting at the table.

LLECHEU, SON OF ARTHUR, 70: The Lohot who is found in 'The High History of the Holy Grail' where he falls victim to Sir Kay's envy.

LLEIRWG, SON OF COEL, 35,62: The British king, Lucius, who supposedly sent letters to Pope Eleutherius in 189 A.D., asking to be made a Christian.

LLEW, SON OF CYNVARCH, 21,100,118: Legendary brother of Urien and Arawn who appears as King Lot of Lothian in romance, deriving from Leudonus, the eponymous founder of Leudonisia or Lothian. Father of Medrawd (Mordred) in some accounts.

LLEW LLAW GYFES, 81,124: Son of Gwydion by his sister Arianrod. His story is contained in 'Math, Son of Mathonwy' (Mabinogion).

LLEWEI, DAUGHTER OF SEITHWEDD SAIDI, 96.

LLEYN AND EIVIONYDD IN ARVON, 101: Provinces of Gwynedd (North Wales).

LLIAWS, SON OF NWYVRE, 14: Literally, 'Host, son of Firmament'.

LLONIO LLONWEN IN DYFED, 101.

LLOVAS LLAW DINO, 47: The assassin of Urien of Rheged, perhaps hired by Urien's jealous fellow-prince, Morgant.

LLUDD, SON OF BELI, 17,18,20-22,51,53,100: Often confused with Llyr (who, as King Lear, is given as father to Lludd's daughter Creiddylat = Cordelia) and also with Nudd. As Lludd Llaw Ereint ('of the Silver Hand') he equates with Nuadha Airgedlamh, an Irish deity who originates, like Lludd and Nudd, with the early Celtic god Nodons. As the legendary King Lud, Lludd gave his name to London (Caer-Lud) and also Ludgate.

LLYR LLEDIAITH, 17,18,24,35,36,38,41,49,53, 55,61,99,124: Father of Bran, Bronwen and Manawydan. Little is known of Llyr, whose name, from the Irish 'ler' or 'lir' denotes simply 'sea'. His origin in Ireland is also reflected in the epithet 'Llediaith', 'half-formed speech', which carries the meaning of a language spoken with a strong regional dialect.

LLYR MERINI, 94: Cognate with Llyr (above).

LLYR THE BELLIPOTENT, 29: Llyr Llwydawc.
Either Llyr (above) or, perhaps, Lludd.

LLYWARCH THE AGED, 38,112,116: Llywarch
Hen, son of Elidir Llydanwyn, poet and sometime
chieftain of the northern territories. He is supposed
to have lost his sons in battle, and his lands, and
passed the remainder of his life as a melancholic
poet. He is reputed to have lived for 150 years.

MADAWG MORVRYN, 98: Father of Merddin
Wyllt, and descendant of Coel.

MADAWG, SON OF BRWYN, 77: A descendant of
Cynedda Wledig.

MADAWG, SON OF MEDRON, 61: Otherwise
'Mabon, son of Modron'; the Celtic deities Maponus
(Son) and Matrona (Mother). Their myth seems to
have concerned the abduction of Maponus and his
later restoration to Matrona (see Gair). Late ver-
sions of the myth give Arthur or Cai as his deliverer.

MADOG, SON OF OWAIN, 10: According to one
account, a Welsh prince of the twelfth century who
sailed westward and discovered America.

MADOG MIN, 22: Bishop of Bangor who betrayed
Prince Llewelyn in 1021 A.D., and his grandfather
likewise some time before.

MAEL, SON OF MENWAED, 29.

MAELGWN, FATHER OF RHUN, 25,64: King of
Gwynedd and descendant of Cynedda. The
'Maglocunus' reproached by Gildas for his sinful
behaviour. He may have died in the Yellow Plague,
c.547 A.D.

MAEN DU IN ARVON, 101: Literally, 'Black
Stone'.

MAENARCH, STONE OF, 60.

MAES GWENITH, 101: Literally, 'Wheat Field'.

MALAEN, HORSE OF, 11: If this reference is
taken as meaning a foreign invasion, *vide* Julius

Caesar (Meinlas) and Hengist and Horsa ('Stallion' and 'Horse').

MANAW, 86: The Isle of Man.

MANAWYDAN, SON OF LLYR, 38,124: Brother of Bran and Bronwen. His story is found in 'Manawydan, Son of Llyr' (Mabinogion). The name, like that of the Irish god Mananaan mac Lir, derives from 'Manaw' (above). 'Manawyda' can also mean 'awl', and may account for the title of 'Golden Shoe Wearer' and his role of 'cobbler' in the Mabinogion narrative.

MANDUBRATIUS, SON OF LLUDD, 18,20-22, 51,100: Given in variant Triads as Avarwy, and in Geoffrey of Monmouth's History as Androgeus. For a first-hand account of Mandubratius's teaching, see 'The Gallic War' of Julius Caesar.

MANUBA, 12.

MARCH, SON OF MEIRCHION, 68,101,102,113: The name has been translated as 'Horse, son of Horses' and as 'Marcus, son of Marcianus'. Traditionally, March is King Mark of Cornwall, appearing in the Arthurian cycles with Iseult (Essylt) and Trystan.

MARCHELL, 101: Probably March (above).

MATH, SON OF MATHONWY, 90: A powerful enchanter, whose story 'Math, Son of Mathonwy' is found in the Mabinogion. Uncle of Gwydion and Arianrod.

MATHOLWCH THE IRISHMAN, 49: Irish king whose ill-treatment of Bronwen led to the battle in which he was killed and Bran fatally wounded.

MATHRAVAEL, 126: Capital of the ninth century kingdom of Powys.

MAXIMUS, 14,17,21,62: Spanish-born Magnus Maximus, elected Emperor of Rome by troops in Britain, c.382 A.D. He held Gaul for some years, but was eventually taken at Aquilea and executed 388 A.D. Traditionally he was supposed to have denuded Britain of its fighting men, leaving it open to invaders. A romantic account of Maximus is found in 'The Dream of Macsen Wledic' (Mabinogion).

MEDERAI, DAUGHTER OF PADELLVAWR, 96.

MEDRAWD or MEDROD, 20,21,51,52,100,118: The son of Llew or, in other accounts, the nephew-son of Arthur. Better known as Mordred, who usurped the kingdom left in his charge while Arthur marched on Rome, and abducted (or seduced) Guinevere. Arthur returned to Britain and there followed the fatal battle of Camlan. An entry in the 'Annales Cambriae' for 537 A.D. records 'the action of Camlann where Arthur and Medraut fell', but gives no indication as to whether they opposed each other or fought on the same side against a common enemy.

MEDROD, 45,50: See Medrawd (above).

MEIRIADOG, 14: An ancient north-east division of Powys.

MENW THE AGED, 93.

MENW, SON OF TEIRGWAEDD, 90: Magician, shape-shifter, who could confer invisibility and transform himself to a bird. He is featured in the story of 'Culhwch and Olwen' (Mabinogion).

MENWAED OF ARLLECHWEDD, 101.

MERDDIN, BARD OF EMRYS, 10,125: Named Merlin Ambrosius to distinguish him from Merddin Wyllt. A composite figure containing elements of Ambrosius, originally credited with Merlin's encounter with Vortigern, and Merddin Wyllt. Geoffrey of Monmouth is largely responsible for the creation, and for the attribution of magical powers which have led to the familiar image of 'Merlin the Magician' today.

MERDDIN, SON OF MADAWG MORVRYN, 125: Known as Merddin Wyllt (='the Wild'), Merlin Silvestris (='of the Woods') or Merlin Calidonius (= 'of the Wood of Celidon'). The prophecies attributed to him, concerning the future of the Britons, enjoyed great vogue in the twelfth century when the cultus of Arthur was reaching its peak. Geoffrey of Monmouth, the creator of Merlin (above), also wrote a Life of Merlin based on Merddin Wyllt. There is some reason to suppose he was an historical bard of the sixth century.

MERVIN, KING OF MATHRAVAEL, 43: King of Powys, with his capital at Mathravael, ruling in the late ninth century. A son of Rhodri the Great.

MONSTER OF BANNAWG, 95: Possibly the giant who was 'excavated' by St. Cadoc whilst clearing the ground for his new monastery near the mountain of Bannawc. The giant revealed himself as Caw of Prydyn, once a king beyond the mountains.

MONSTER OF EDNYVEDAWG DRYTHYLL, 95.

MONSTER OF MELAN, 95.

MORDAV THE GENEROUS, 30: A prince of the north, contemporary with Rhydderch.

MORDDAL, ARTIST OF CERAINT, 91.

MORGAN THE GREATLY COURTEOUS, 31,42, 118: Morgan Mwynvawr. In legend, the owner of one of the thirteen treasures of Britain: a chariot which would convey the owner to whatever place he wished to go. He has also been proposed as the eponymous founder of Glamorgan (Gwlad-Morganwg), or the jealous prince, Morgant, who sought Urien's death.

MORIEN WITH THE BEARD, 44.

MORVRAN, SON OF TEGID, 83: Cognate with Affagdu, the hideous child of Ceridwen. Literally, 'Great Raven'.

MORVYDD, DAUGHTER OF URIEN, 102: Sister

of Owain, likewise born (according to legend) from
the liaison of Urien and a princess of Annwfn.

MWRCHAN THE THIEF, 124.

MYNOGAN or MANOGAN, 8,11,14,17: Father of
Beli.

MYNYDDAWG EIDDIN, 79: Mynyddawg was
leader of the ill-fated combined expedition which
fought the Saxons at Cattraeth. Probably a nick-
name or title with military connotations applied to
Aeddan, king of Dal Riada.

NANHWYNAIN, 20.

NUDD THE GENEROUS, 30,79,85: Nudd Hael.
Given, in one genealogy, as father of Gwendolleu,
and thus a contemporary of Rhydderch and Urien
in the last half of the sixth century. Nudd, the
father of Gwyn, mentioned in Triad 89, is an older,
mythical figure, equating with Lludd and derived
from the early god of the Celts, Nodons or Nodens.

NWYDD NAV NEIVION, 97: Builder of the ship
which preserved Dwyvan and Dwyvach from the
Deluge. He has been compared with Noah, Neptune
and the Irish Nemed, who is said to have colonised
Ireland after the Flood.

NWYVRE, 14: Literally, 'Sky', 'Space', 'Firma-
ment'. The consort of Arianrod, surviving in name
only.

OETH AND ANOETH, 61: The fortress-prison
which held the captive Gair. According to a legend
found in Iolo Morganwg's manuscripts this maze-
like prison was constructed of human bones by
Manawydan.

ORDOVICES, 16: The tribe which occupied the
north-western parts of Wales at the time of the
Roman conquest.

OWAIN, SON OF AMBROSIUS, 34,41,53: From
the context of Triad 34, identical with Owain the

son of Maximus mentioned in Triad 21. The claim of Triad 53, that he buried Bran's head, does not tally with the account given in the Mabinogion.

OWAIN, SON OF MAXIMUS, 17,21: History records only one son of Maximus, Victor. Owain, however, has entered legend as a knight who died battling with a giant after both had hurled steel balls at the other in the course of the combat.

OWAIN, SON OF URIEN, 25,40,105: Prince of the northern kingdom of Rheged, active in the last part of the sixth century. Owain was a celebrated hero, later assumed into Arthurian legend as Yvain and popularly credited as the son of a princess of Annwfn.

PADARN, 19: St. Padarn or Paternus.

PADROGYL, 117: The Cornish St. Petroc, son of the Dumnonian prince Clement. He is sometimes given as one of the *seven* survivors of Camlan.

PASGEN, SON OF URIEN, 74: No record survives to explain his reputation for arrogance, and it may be that Pascent(ius), the rebellious son of Vortigern in Geoffrey's History, is the source for this claim.

PENARWEN, WIFE OF OWAIN, 105.

PENDARAN OF DYFED, 16,101: The title accorded to Pwyll, father of Pryderi, after he had ruled Annwfn for a year in place of Arawn. 'Great Lord'.

PENRHYN PENWEDIG, 101: Land's End, Cornwall. In variant Triads, Penrhyn Austin is substituted.

PEREDUR, SON OF ELEUVER, 81: A renowned hero who fought at Arderydd against Gwendolleu, 573 A.D., and who died some years later fighting the Saxons.

PEREDUR, SON OF EVRAWG, 121: Prototype of the Sir Percival of Arthurian romance who achieves a vision of the Holy Grail in company with Bors and

Galahad. The story of 'Peredur' (Mabinogion) contains non-Christian elements, however, and draws on earlier Quest material. He is unlikely to equate with Peredur (above), invariably paired with his brother Gwrgi, although his father, Evrawg (='York'), suggests a similarly northern origin.

PERWYR, DAUGHTER OF RHUN RYSEDDVAWR, 106.

PHARAON, FORTRESS OF, 53: Dinas Ffaraon Dandde, later known as Dinas Emrys, near Beddgelert in Caernarvonshire. The two dragons, one red, one white, represented the race of Britons and a foreign race striving to overcome them. They were exposed at the close of Vortigern's reign by the boy Ambrosius or, alternatively, the young Merlin.

PLENYDD, 58,92: Primary bard. Literally, 'Shining'.

PLOT OF THE LONG KNIVES, 20: See 'Plot of Stonehenge'.

PLOT OF STONEHENGE, 60: The assassination of the British nobility and battle-leaders, organised by the Saxon commander Hengist, when they met with Saxon mercenaries at Stonehenge under truce. Only Eidiol and Vortigern escaped with their lives, the former by his prowess, the latter to conclude a humiliating agreement with the enemy.

PRINCE LLEWELYN, 22: The last prince of North Wales. The allusion, however, is to Llewelyn, son of Seisyllt, who usurped the throne from Aedan Blegored in 1015 A.D., and who was killed in 1021 A.D.

PRYDAIN, SON OF AEDD THE GREAT, 1-4,34, 36,54,55,59: Eponymous founder of Ynys Prydain, the Isle of Britain, and therefore comparable to the Brut, or Brutus, of Geoffrey of Monmouth's History.

PRYDERI, SON OF DOLER, 75: 'Care' son of 'Grief'.

PRYDERI, SON OF PWYLL, 101: A central figure of the Mabinogion sequence. His abduction, shortly after birth, from his mother Rhiannon makes him comparable to Gair and Mabon.

PRYDYN, 69: 'Pictland'.

PWYL, 7: Poland.

PYBYDD THE BALD, 99.

RHEGED: The most important of the sixth century northern kingdoms. The precise extent is unknown, but it seems to have included the lands south of Carlisle down to Lancashire and the North Riding of Yorkshire.

RHINERI, SON OF TANGWYN, 75.

RHITTA GAWR, 54,55: Rhitta the Giant. Something of a hero in the Triads, he is elsewhere depicted as an oppressor himself. In Geoffrey of Monmouth's account Rhitta is killed by King Arthur, who takes the robe of beards and adds the giant's own to it.

RHIWALLON, SON OF URIEN, 27.

RHIWALLON OF THE BROOM-(BUSH)-HAIR, 28,70: Rhiwallon Gwallt Banadlen. Folk-lore preserves the legend of Rhiwallon who was instructed in the use of herbs by his lake-dwelling mother, the lady of Llyn y Van Vach.

RHIWGYVERTHWCH, 101: The Hill of Cyferthwch.

RHODRI THE GREAT, 59,126: Rhodri Mawr, ninth century ruler who became king of all Wales before his death in 877 A.D.

RHOREI THE GREAT, 96.

RHOSS, 12.

RHUDDLUM, 90: Correctly, 'the Dwarf'; a possible variant of Gwyddolwyn; 'Culhwch and Olwen'.

RHUN, SON OF BELI, 31: From the context of
Triad 31, Rhun son of Maelgwn.
RHUN, SON OF EINIAWN, 74: Probably Rhun
son of Maelgwn, and brother of Einiawn.
RHUN, SON OF MAELGWN, 25,28: Mid-sixth
century king of Gwynedd. After his lands were
attacked by a confederation of northern princes,
Rhun marched his army northwards in an impres-
sive display of power. The loyalty of his followers
became legendary.
RHUVON THE FAIR, SON OF GWYDDNAW
GARANHIR, 77.
RHUVON THE FAIR, SON OF DEWRATH
WLEDIG, 25: Probably cognate with Rhuvon
(above); mentioned in 'The Dream of Rhonabwy'
(Mabinogion).
RHYDDERCH THE GENEROUS, 30,52,106: Mid-
sixth century northern ruler of the region of
Strathclyde. He owned one of the thirteen treasures
of Britain: a sword which burst into flame if any
but he drew it.
RHYHAWD, SON OF MORGANT, 113,123: 'Vain
bard' should be interpreted as 'amateur', i.e., as
with Arthur and Caswallawn, bardism was not
Rhyhawd's main occupation.
RIANNON, 124: Rhiannon, wife of Pwyll and then
of Manawydan. Identified with Rigantona ('The
Great Queen'), an early Celtic deity. Arianrod was
the mother of Llew Llaw Gyfes; Rhiannon, of
Pryderi.
ROWENA, 37,51,53,100: See Alis Ronwen.
ST. DAVID, 19,64: Dewi, patron saint of Wales. In
the first half of the sixth century he was instru-
mental in defeating the Pelagian heresy in Wales. As
the Primate of Wales he removed his see from
Caerleon to Menevia (Mynyw), before his death in
544 A.D.

SANDDE ANGEL-ASPECT, 83: This Triad is
recorded in 'Culhwch and Olwen' (Mabinogion).
SAWYL THE LOFTY-HEADED, 74: Sawyl
Benuchel. A confusing figure, sometimes given as
the father-in-law of Maelgwn or as a contemporary
of Urien. The earth swallowed him when he
opposed St. Cadoc, but he also fathered a saint,
Asaph. To complete the confusion, he is alterna-
tively given as Sawyl Penissel, 'the Low-headed'.
SEA-GIRT GREEN SPACE, 1: 'Clas Merdin',
usually translated as 'Merlin's Precinct'.
SEITHYNIN, SON OF SEITHYN SAIDA, 37:
Custodian of the embankment of Cantre'r Gwaelod,
in charge of the dyke gates which were opened to
let the river flow through, and closed to keep out
the tides.
SELYV, SON OF CYNAN GARWYN, 76.
SILURIA, 14,16,37: That part of southern Wales,
in the region of the Usk valley, once occupied by
the Silures.
TALIESIN, 47,73,125: Sixth century bard. A body
of his work survives, including 'The Spoils of
Annwfn', giving several references to non-Christian
myths. A mythical Taliesin, born of Ceridwen, is
the subject of the 'Hanes Taliesin', translated by
Lady Charlotte Guest in her edition of the
Mabinogion.
TEGAU EURVRON, 103,108: Tegau 'Gold Breast',
whose mantle for chaste women was one of the
thirteen treasures of Britain.
TEILAW, 19,93: St. Teilo, sixth century bishop
with his principal monastery at Llandeilo Fawr.
THEODOSIUS, 56.
TINWAED THE CRUTCHED, 75: More properly,
Dunawt. 'Crutched' may be interpreted as 'bearing
a crook', either as shepherd or ecclesiastic.
TRISTVARDD, 40: In other accounts, the son of

Morgant and the bard of Urien.

TRYSTAN, SON OF TALLWCH, 32,69,78,101,102, 105,113: Better known, from Arthurian romance, as Sir Trystan (or Tristram), nephew of King Mark, lover of Iseult. His name may originate with Drust, son of the Pictish king Tallorc, active in the third quarter of the eighth century. Triad 113 mistakenly gives him as the son of March.

TRYWYL, 103: 'Treul the Blameless'.

TYDAIN, 57,92,93: His grave, in the region of Bron Aren, is mentioned in 'The Black Book of Carmarthen'.

UR(B) WITH THE MIGHTY HOST, 8,14: Unidentified. The name, in conjunction with that of his servant Mathata, suggests an Irish source for the story.

URIEN OF RHEGED, 25,27,40,47,72,102,105: Son of Cynvarch. A powerful sixth century king of the north Britons, active c.570-590 A.D. He appears to have been murdered whilst leading an alliance of British forces against the Saxons, at the instigation of his fellow-prince, Morgant. Urien, as father of Owain-Yvain, enters Arthurian legend as King Uryence.

UTHYR PENDRAGON, 90: Brother of Ambrosius and father of Arthur. Uthyr's epithet, 'Chief Dragon', may have a military significance, but there is little to indicate whether he was an historical or legendary figure.

VLEIDUR VLAM, 114: Mentioned in 'Culhwch and Olwen' (Mabinogion).

VORTIGERN, 9,14,20,21,37,53,100: Gwyrthern, the principal villain of the Triads, active c.425-459 A.D. His recruitment of Saxon mercenaries, following an established precedent set by the Romans, seems to have been forced on him by the large-scale emigration of Britons to Brittany in the first part of the fifth century. This, combined with the removal of troops by both Maximus and Constantine III, left Britain in poor shape to cope with Irish, Pictish and sea-going marauders who were drawn to the rich lowlands after the collapse of the Roman power. Despite the initial success of Vortigern's policy, the Saxons were soon tempted to turn on their former employers, and so began the process which eventually drove the Britons back into Cornwall and Wales. As the instigator of all ensuing disaster Vortigern has been charged with a variety of crimes: treachery, murder, usurpation, heresy, incest and drunkenness to name but some. In legend he died a suitably horrible death, by fire, on the accession of Ambrosius. It is possible, however, that he in fact crossed to France and confounded his detractors by achieving spiritual eminence under the name of St. Gwrthiern.

WILLIAM THE BASTARD, 12: William the Conqueror.

YSGAVNELL, 39,46: See Gall.

YSTRE GYVAELWG, 14: Probert suggests a region in Normandy.

BIBLIOGRAPHY

Trioedd Ynys Prydein: The Welsh Triads — Rachel
Bromwich — University of Wales Press, 1961

The Mabinogion — trans. G. Jones and T. Jones —
Everyman, 1949

Four Ancient Books of Wales — W.F. Skene —
Edinburgh, 1868

Celtic Myth and Legend — Charles Squire —
Gresham Publishing Co. Ltd.

Myths and Legends of the Celtic Race —
T.W. Rolleston — George G. Harrap & Co., 1911

The History of the Kings of Britain —
Geoffrey of Monmouth — Various editions

The Lives of the Welsh Saints — G.H. Doble —
University of Wales Press, 1971

The Age of Arthur — John Morris — Weidenfeld and
Nicolson, 1973